JUST BECAUSE
WE ARE THE 99%

Also by Miss Mary

Just Because the President is Black

JUST BECAUSE WE ARE THE 99%

By Historic Observer—Miss Mary

TRAFFORD
PUBLISHING

Printed in the United States of America.

ISBN: 978-1-4669-1916-7 (sc)
ISBN: 978-1-4669-1917-4 (hc)
ISBN: 978-1-4669-1915-0 (e)

Library of Congress Control Number: 2012904439

Trafford rev. 03/20/2012

 www.trafford.com

North America & International
toll-free: 1 888 232 4444 (USA & Canada)
phone: 250 383 6864 ✦ fax: 812 355 4082

ACKNOWLEDGMENTS

I am so grateful for those who enjoyed my first book and encouraged me to write this second book

To my husband, Richard, who loved my first book and told me to keep writing since I still have plenty of time on my hands. To my daughter, Kimberly, who is so busy that I feel guilty having her as my editor-in-chief, but she's cheap. To my son, Killis, who I hope has read my first book. To my mom, Ruth, who is my second editor-in-chief and is extremely efficient in editing my book. To my sister, Barbara, who was so excited about my first book that she encouraged me to write my second book. To Joe, Don, Kyra, Karla, and Vincent, who are busy but will read my books soon. To my grands, Sanjseeray, Richard Oree, and grandnephew, Prescott, who are too young to understand yet but will have my books as the real history of this remarkable time. To my father, Killis Benjamin, in loving memory.

TABLE OF CONTENTS

Acknowledgments v
Foreword... 1

A Little Something.. 4
Year 2011 6
It's on Us, Buddy.. 11
It's the Economy, Stupid.. 16
Jobs, What Jobs?... 23
Legislators from Hell... 32
Way To Go, 99% 43
I Sure Hope You're Satisfied... 48
State of the Union... 57
You can Trust Me 60
Oops, Wrong Turn 64
It's a Deal 66
Pay Up or Else... 69
It's a Private Matter 75
Foreign Affairs... 81
Give it a Rest... 86
The Pledge 90
Think of Something... 93
All My Children.. 99
We Voted for That... 103
And So It Goes... 107
It's Racism, Seriously 109
Turning in the Right Direction 112
Let's Pretend.. 118

Afterword... 123
Endnotes.. 125

FOREWORD

It's 2011 and things have become so much worse. Wow! Who didn't see that coming? Apparently, the 99% didn't see it coming. How was it possible for the 99% to miss all of the signs? Well, it really does not matter because I will say what I have to say no matter what. Americans are 100% responsible for where we are and where we will be in the future. That's right, the 99% is 100% responsible for everything. Where did I hear that? Oh, that's right, I said that in my last book, *Just Because the President is Black*. Well, I'm back! Events had not improved what so ever and I still had time on my hands. When the 99% played the "I want to put more Republicans in office so that we can have more jobs and bipartisanship" card and pretended that they were serious, I knew that the 99% was about to pay the piper for their racism, their inattentiveness, and their foolishness. I felt, with this book and the last book, that it was my responsibility to show the 99% the error of their ways and get a good laugh in the process. Now, I know everyone will say that I am being insensitive to those who are losing their homes or those who are jobless and that is not true. However, when the 99% sat back and allowed those in office to jerk them around while that same 99% divided itself and did nothing, we ended up where we are and where we will be in the future. When we pretended the equal blame game and refused to see the enemies of our democracy, we did ourselves an injustice. Our Congress is totally fractured and that is because of many people's desire to punish this President. Therefore, we are in for a hard future and we will be totally responsible because we did not connect the President's failing with the 99% failing.

Throughout this book and my last book, I refer to the 99% as lazy, stupid, nothings. We are lazy because we refuse to fully participate in the democratic process by validating facts that are presented to us and holding politicians accountable for how they represent us. We are stupid because we doggedly defend the inaccuracies that we did not verify as they were proven false. We become nothings because we allow the controlling 1% to continually manipulate us with ease for their gain while we gain nothing.

We divide and the controlling minority, the ignorant, the intolerant, the selfish, take your pick, get and keep control.

The middle class, aka 99%, could have been on the road to economic recovery a long time ago. All we had to do was insist that our political parties worked for our benefit and resolved the situations. We could be buying houses, cars, and, of course, shoes. All those who said "NO," or refused to cooperate in our recovery, should have been sent home, simple and easy. That is the way a majority operates in the best of times. That is the way a majority shows politicians that they are the ones in charge. That is the way the majority acts like the 99%. Alas, that did not happen. However long we are in this recession will be on our backs. However long we continue to be unemployed will be on our backs. However long we continue to lose our homes will be on our backs. We voted for dissension in 2010 just because the President is Barack Obama. We voted to place more Republicans, who were responsible for the huge debt that we are presently in, back in office. We either voted for those changes or we refused to vote, which is the same as voting for those changes. The 99% has placed itself in so much manure, it makes me laugh. It makes me laugh because conning the 99% is always easy when there is a reason to be conned. A black man is the best reason ever. Unfortunately, now the 99% will be spending from 2011 to forever cleaning up the mess it has placed itself in and will deserve everything that happens.

Once again, I will perform my duty as the old, know-it-all, black woman and remind everyone why we are where we are and how we got there. So, here we go again with my observations and opinions, which are backed up by my favorite know-it-all site, GOOGLE. I will emphasize how racism has been effective in diluting the goals of the 99%. Barack Obama's term, as President of the United States, is the best example of responsive racism that any of us has seen in a long time. It has provided an effective distraction to the strategies employed by the 1% in maintaining their unfair percentage of wealth and power. We are literally cutting off our noses to spite our faces. Young people will probably wonder why I am talking about our noses but older Americans will understand. It simply means that because of racist attitudes and the refusal to understand the true target, we bring about the worst for ourselves and keep fluctuating between good times and bad times.

In my last book, I was gentle or at least I thought I was (mom laughing). I tried to be as respectful as possible (husband laughing). I resorted to name calling and I felt I was still respectful (daughter and sister laughing). However, this book, which will be about 2011 only, is not intended to be as gentle as my previous book (whole family laughing). The forces of destruction are in full force. I am required to stand toe to toe with evil. Ha-ha, that is just a small taste of my witticism. I will call a spade a spade. That probably was not the correct terminology being as the President is black, but as they say at the Olympics, "Let the games begin."

A Little Something

In the fall of 2011, Bank of America decided to try and bitch slap the 99% by adding a $5 fee for using their debit cards.[1] Debit cards are our checking accounts in plastic form. In other words, Bank of America was trying to make money on our checking accounts, of which they pay practically no interest. While our checking accounts sit in their banks, they use our money at their disposal. If Bank of America had gotten away with this tiny maneuver, other banks would have followed suit and we would continue being abused by our banks. However, the 99% started complaining and more importantly they started moving their money. Nothing says "I don't like your treatment of me" like goodbye. As a result, Bank of America and the other money suckers, oops, I mean other banks, decided not to charge that debit fee. Hooray, hooray! The 99% experienced their first moment of unity and got results. Hooray! Where are our cheerleaders? "We are the 99%, We are the 99%, Rah, Rah, Rah" (giggles).

The Occupy Wall Street group appears to be our second best moment of unity, so far. Their declaration of being the 99% is what this book is about. Okay, it's also about President Barack Obama because he campaigned on helping the 99%. All that has occurred, after his election, has only been about the attempt by the 1% to increase their wealth and maintain control through their paid henchmen, Republicans. I thought I would be old and senile before the 99% understood that they were the real targets. (I know, I know, you are saying I am old but I am not senile, yet. I am, however, writing as fast as I can, just in case.) Historically, a black man in charge has always guaranteed a split in the 99%. If I know this and I am not running for office, surely politicians know this. When the Tea Party started, many thought that they were the 99%. Not me, of course, because I have already established myself as a know-it-all. Once I saw them fighting against the Affordable Health Care Initiative and working with the the healthcare industry, I knew that this group of people was being manipulated by the 1%. Think about what the Tea Party was saying. They felt that 40 million of the 99%, including many of themselves, did not deserve proper healthcare. They should just die. However, the Tea Party fooled a lot of the 99% and were elected into office only to become hostage takers on most bills and the biggest irritants the 99% has ever seen. Now, hopefully, we have the true 99%. They are rallying against Wall Street, who was the initiator of our economic demise. FOX News, of course, has terrible things to say about this 99% and who did not see that coming? The Occupy Wall Street group wants shared sacrifice from the 1% and that is definitely not the agenda of Republicans or FOX News.

Just because we are the 99%, we must understand our true power. We must convince those who are waffling, just because the President is black, into joining the revolution. That's right, I said the revolution because at this time in our history, the 1% has all of our tax money and many of our politicians. We can't do much about our tax money until we reign in our politicians. We have to register to vote. We must move into districts that have been set up to manipulate our votes. We must then vote and recall when necessary. We must pay attention to every bill that our local, state, and Federal Government is dumping on us. We must be involved because we, the 99%, are the real targets and that is not a little something.

YEAR 2011

Year 2011 was pivotal because it was the year that the 99% appeared to finally wake up. Everything that happened in year 2011 was about President Obama's failing, because of race, and about the 99% failing with President Obama. Sorry 99%, President Obama was not the only target, you were also. In order for everyone to appreciate my wisdom, it is imperative that everyone identify those who are the 99%. The Republican base, which is about 30%, is a part of the 99% not the 1%, sorry about that. Even all of the commentators and contributors on FOX News, who appear to hate the 99%, are not a part of the 1%. It makes those individuals look really really stupid, sorry about that. Cuban Americans, of the 13% Hispanics, are a part of the 99% not the 1%. The immigration policy that will affect Mexican Americans will also affect Cuban Americans, sorry about that. The 1% of the 12% of African Americans who think that the Republican party is an inclusive party, good luck on that. When Ann Coulter made the statement "Our Blacks are better that their Blacks,"[1] it pretty much showed that 1% how much they are not included in the party, sorry about that. Women are more that 50% of the voters in this country.[2] Republican women should really pay attention to the way the male members of their party vote to eliminate anything related to women. All women need to understand that no woman will ever be considered in the 1%. Women will always be in the 99%, sorry about that. The 50% or more who have been convinced that the country is going in the wrong direction must believe that the Republican's plan of no shared sacrificing is going to take the 99% in the right direction. However, Republicans are really only taking the 1% in the right direction, sorry about that.

The results of the 2010 midterm elections came to fruition in 2011. We elected the chaos, so we cannot complain. That's why I'm laughing when I hear so many commentators state that Republicans over reached. Republicans told the 99% exactly what they were going to do, over and over again. Where were you, 99%? Didn't you hear the rhetoric of tax cuts and spending cuts? Didn't you hear the rhetoric about never, ever working with this President? Did you think it would not involve you? The year

2011 was all about us going back into the ditch, which was the place we were when George W. Bush left office.[3] We made that 2010 decision just because Barack Obama is the President.

I want everyone to try and think back to 2009. I know that will be difficult for some and really difficult for me. Older Americans like to stay in present day, safer that way for the aging brain, but let's all try together. The "Too big to fail" corporations, tying up over 63% of the Gross Domestic Products (GDP),[4] were failing. The response was the Troubled Asset Relief Program (TARP) which was signed into law by President George W. Bush in October 2008, a full month before Barack Obama was even elected.[5] The President inherited huge debts and deficits, a collapsing housing market, a world wide financial crisis, and TARP.[6] However, that did not stop Republicans from blaming the President for TARP and complaining about bailing out those "Too big to fail" companies.[7] Those who believed Republicans did not understand that the only repercussion of allowing those companies to fail would have been record unemployment. Republicans knew, and so did I, that those "Too big to fail" corporations would have filed bankruptcy which would have translated into the company keeping their monies and firing the 99%. So, let's not get it twisted (I love that new saying) because the 99% was always the Republican's target with potentially record unemployment. Here is the best part. Republicans blamed the President for the economic disaster that he inherited. They blamed him for the slow recovery as they refused to participate in that recovery. In 2010, they gained the momentum and were returned to office.

Now, I am trying very hard not to laugh at American's foolish behavior. However, everyone must know that the controlling 1% and their henchmen, Republicans, are laughing their fool heads off at the ease of controlling the 99%. Think about it for a minute. We returned those who were responsible for the economic disaster, those who refused to help clean up the disaster, back into office, in under two years. Just to completely make fools of ourselves, we placed more of those same, "We will do nothing to help you" individuals into state houses and governorships. Priceless, absolutely priceless! Okay, I am laughing just a little bit because these divide and conquer techniques have worked for years and they always work best when race is an issue. Hopefully, the 99% is waking up.

As I said before, the 99% is 100% responsible for where we are and where we will be in the future. Who knew that my predictions about the future would come true in 2011? I thought I would have had at least another year of unbelievable lies and insinuations before those in charge came after the 99% full force. I thought the 99% could, at least, pretend until November 2012. Who knew that Republicans would seriously allow their crazies to come to the surface and become the face of the party? Who knew so many of the 99% would follow so stupidly? It's actually embarrassing to watch. You know the old saying and I love old sayings, "If you dance with the Devil, the Devil will own your soul." Okay, I seriously made that up, but it sounds like the Republican party to me. Republicans have let their crazies out into the open. They are telling everyone who will listen that they will do everything for the 1% and we had better take it or we get stuck with the Black President. They have told everyone that this President will be a one-term president and that is their first agenda.[8] Their real agenda, however, is spending cuts and no tax increases because the 1% must be protected. I watched the 2011 Republican Iowa Presidential Debate. All of the Republican contenders raised their hands and stated that even if they were presented with a bill that had ten spending cuts to one tax increase, they would not vote for the bill.[9] Translation: Republicans will cut Medicare, Medicaid, Social Security, Education, infrastructure repairs, women programs, children programs, veteran programs, and any and all programs that ONLY affect the 99%, before they ask for any increased revenue from the 1%. Ha-ha, I have to laugh here because the only reason Republicans can be this brazen, knowing that the 99% wants shared sacrifice, is because the President is black and they can split the 99% over their hidden racism. They can blame him for the sun not shinning and many of the 99% believe every word just because the President is black.

Many of the 99% have pretended not to notice the detrimental rhetoric and its effect on the 99%. That is what subconscious racism does to people, it makes them duplicitous in their own demise (Wow! That was one hell of an intelligent sounding statement, I am impressed with myself). My point is that we know that a great deal of what we hear is misinformation. The Occupy Wall Street group, or 99% as they like to call themselves, are the real 99% who are fed up with our mistreatment and, in the process, are being maligned with a lot of misinformation. They are young and old, teachers and executives, union and nonunion, liberal and conservatives, and working and non working families. However, the master liars, FOX News and Republicans, have labeled this 99% as domestic terrorists,"[10] potheads, ignorant, homeless criminals, left-wing agitators, aging anarchist, Nazi, and communists.[11] That is really harsh, detrimental, and meant to misinform. Wait a minute, didn't FOX News and the Tea Party call President Obama some type of communist or Nazi, just to misinform? I hope the 99% is paying attention to all of these attempts at division through lies and misinformation.

Year 2011 showed the Republican's disregard for the 99%. There were no blurred lines. Many of the 99% thought, that even though Republicans told them that their only concern was the 1%, they were just kidding. How many times did I hear voters state that because they did not get everything from President Obama, and everything was not back to normal in two years, they would vote for Republicans. That would be those same Republicans who were responsible for the deregulation that triggered the economic disaster.[12] That would be those same Republicans who left us unpaid for wars, unpaid for programs, and deficit producing tax cuts.[13] That would be those same Republicans who endorsed the Ryan, kill Medicare, Budget Bill, the "No new taxes on the wealthy no matter what" pledge, and the Cut, Cap, and Balance Bill, which would send the 99% to the poor house quickly.[14] How many times did I hear some of the 99% state that the country is going in the wrong direction? As if going with the Republican agenda, of the 99% sacrificing everything and the 1% sacrificing nothing, is the right direction. Didn't we just live through those economic times from 2000-2008?

I did not think that I would live to see the end results of that foolish 2010 decision but I am still here and laughing like a person at a black Comedy Club. The 99% will have to learn to hate this President, but not let that hate affect their life, aka, cutting off their noses to spite their faces. At least, until we are back in the black, which does not mean more blacks in your life, calm down, it just means back on the positive side of the ledger.

If 2011 does not show the 99% what this is all about, then nothing on this planet will make them admit the truth about the ease of being duped because of race. If the 99% is really that easy to be duped, then I have some Everglades property that I would like to sell to those who made that 2010 decision. I will list it on Ebay. My point is that 2011 has shown us that when we divide our 99%, it makes us easy pickings for the controlling 1%. It has validated the President's remarks about Republicans taking the economy back into the ditch, which is exactly where we went in the year 2011. However, there is one fact that can not be missed and that fact is quite simple. If this President had been a white man, there is no way that Republicans would have gotten away with this level of disrespect and so much misinformation. The 99% would not have had any confusion about Republicans being the responsible party, no way. Miraculously, the 99% would have been able to see those who had no love for them and probably would not be in the streets marching claiming their 99%. Fascinating, isn't it? (Yes, I am laughing.)

Just because we are the 99%, all pretense must cease to exist. We must use year 2011 as an example of what not to do if we ever have any chance of a true democracy. There can be no more "I didn't know all of this was happening," "This is the way all presidents are treated," "It's the way the opposing party acts," It's American politics, not racism." Excuses, excuses, and no chance of common sense entering the room. I write these books for several reasons and those reasons are to place all of the events together, to make people think, and for my grands, of course. So, let's put all of the events together so we can have hard examples of how the 99% has acted just because the President is black and just because we are so divided. These events will be both shocking and insulting. It will definitely be the only America that 12% of the 99%, like myself, have ever known. So, let's start year 2011.

It's on Us, Buddy

For two books now, I have made the accusation that the 99% is responsible for everything. Why do I keep saying that we are 100% responsible? Why do I keep placing the blame on the 99%? I do this because those who do not pay attention to history are doomed to repeat it. I do this because the mistakes we have made come back to haunt us and we are being haunted now. We continue to elect those who promise and never deliver. Then we leave them in office forever. We watch as our politicians are influenced by special interest and we are never their true interest. We allow racism, sexism, homophobia, and other isms to dictate our paths. We eliminate many of the best people with our predetermined prejudices. We have ignored our 99% advantage for years and stayed divided. However, we have awaken and I can't wait to see the results in 2012.

With the 2008 election, the 99% gave the impression that they were about to change and embrace the "Equality for all" mantra, that is suppose to be America. However, the controlling 1% went into full blown overdrive to prove that we did not really make that change. A real change would have truly united the 99% and that would not benefit the 1%. With the election of our first Black President, the tactics employed on Black Americans for years became so much more obvious. I can not keep writing books trying to make the 99% understand the foolish behavior they keep repeating over and over again just because the selected person is not the correct race or gender. (I'm no youngster, though I look great, but time is not on my side.) I refuse to keep watching Congress waste time debating bills we have already agreed on and passed years ago. I'm tired of us letting them constantly divide us. I want to enjoy my retirement without the constant threat of government shutdowns, debt ceiling debacles, promised Medicare eliminations, and Social Security overhauls. I want our government to come together and make decisions for us that benefit us. I want our government to present those ideas to all of us and we will vote on what we want, period. I am on the beach five seconds after I vote.

As a nation, we have survived the Great Depression and many recessions along the way. There is more than enough history, information, and experience to show us how to live financially, humanely, and better lives. We never need to disagree on the path to take because we have taken every path and we have the facts of those decisions. However, here we sit with our politicians pretending that they can not make sound economic decisions while they fight over everything. Here we sit with the same old deceptive manipulations that keep our economy fluctuating between bust and boom. Here we sit allowing our representatives to make us suffer, just because the President is Barack Obama and the 99% is so divided. The President warned everyone, before the 2010 midterm elections, that there would be hell to pay if we gave Republicans the keys to the economy back.[1] No one listened. Therefore, the chaos of 2011 is on the 99% and the "NO" party who they voted into office.

Since I am established as the old, know-it-all, black woman, it seems to be up to me to make the tough decisions for this country. It always ends up being on the backs of old people. However, here is the best part, I am not being paid to express my views, truly a bargain. Since history is the best indicator of the future, let's analyze what history has taught us about our economy. We have had quite a few examples, since the 80's, on how to handle our economy. One has worked beautifully and the others have failed miserably. President Clinton's policies of fiscal discipline, eliminating the budget deficit, low interest rates, renewed private sector growth, and tax increases worked beautifully.[2] Twenty-two million jobs were created with his economic strategy and everyone appeared to prosper. So much so, that we had over three billion dollars in surplus.[3] Every other president has produced only deficits with the Republican presidents producing the largest deficits.[4] The reason for those statistics, about large deficits, is because Republicans love Reaganomics. Reaganomics, aka Trickle Down Theory,[5] worked miserably and it is the only economic agenda that Republicans love to embrace. A simple explanation of this theory is that by giving the 1% subsidies, tax breaks, and any method on this planet to make as much money as possible, the 1% will trickle that money down to the 99%. Ha-ha, I'm sorry, I started laughing too soon, so let me finish my explanation. This Trickle Down Theory has been tried by President Reagan, of course thus the name Reaganomics. President George H.W. Bush (Bush I) & President George W Bush (Bush II) also practiced this theory and all three president's national debt rose to record levels. Bush

II produced the highest debt ever with the potential of massive future debt.[6] Republicans will not like to hear this but the debt we are in now, and the debt for the next ten years, will all lead back to President George W. Bush. I certainly hope that the 99% will remember this passage about the massive debt when Republicans try to elect John Ellis Bush (Bush III). The problem with the Trickle Down Theory is that the entire idea rests on the wealthy and corporations sharing their profits with the 99%. Now, I can start laughing hard. As all have seen, and all saw in the previous administrations, many of the 1% do not share, they hoard. A million is not enough and that is why we now have billionaires. Corporations do not hire more people. They simply pay upper management higher salaries and bigger bonuses. Both corporations and the 1% love to move their wealth all over the place just to avoid paying taxes. So, while the theory should be an example of our shared enthusiasm to make America the best she can be, history has shown us that we can not hope for the best and keep getting the shaft, which is where we are at this time in history. When Republicans keep harping on lower taxes and more breaks for the wealthy and corporations, they are telling the 99% that they are foolish and not intelligent enough to pay attention to history. President Clinton convinced Congress to place higher taxes on the wealthy and there were lots and lots of jobs and, guess what, millionaires were still millionaires.[7] Everything that President Clinton did when he was president, okay, maybe not everything, we should be considering now. Even the Republican's beloved president, President Reagan, raised taxes eleven times.[8] Republicans are choosing to ignore history and pretending that facts are not facts, which has been a staple for them for some time.

Why is anyone listening to Republicans telling them how to be economically independent when they have proven that they do not know the pathway to success? Why would we keep following agendas that have been proven not to work? I don't know what the excuse was with the other presidents but I sure know the reason with this President, racism. So, I ask, how stupid are we, I mean, how racist are we? Race has to be the only reason any percentage of the 99% listened and backed a party that made the debt and then blamed the debt on others. Race has to be the only reason the President has to beg Congress to try and put the 99% first and many of the 99% fighting the President on that concept. Race has to be the only reason why the 99% put their trust in those who believe that the only way to save the economy is through cuts to those programs that would benefit the 99%, while allowing the 1% to continue receiving tax breaks and subsidies. At some point, people have to understand that race is responsible for their foolish decisions. Oh, my goodness, are we trying to be responsible and unite in 2011 after we placed more of the "NO" party in office in 2010? Well, better late than never.

Republicans have been working as hard as they can to defeat this President and his attempt to rebuild our economy. Republicans took many racists into their party with their arms wide open.[9] Racists react blindly, consequences be damned. That is the way Republicans and FOX News have behaved. Not one of them has given any thought of their actions or the effect those actions will have on our way of life and our economy. Not one of them care that the 99% is suffering. Not one of them care how the lies and misinformation are leading us into the destruction of this great nation. Their only concern is splitting the 99% into smaller minorities. Their only concern is getting their way on everything and defeating this President. You know Rush Limbaugh's classic phrase, "I hope the President fails."[10] To hell with the country failing. To hell with the 99% failing.

On September 11, 2011, we celebrated our 10th anniversary of 9/11. We united and were a majority on 9/11. Where is that majority now? What keeps us fighting against each other? What is the reason for all of our divisions? Wealthy people were not spared on 9/11 and the same can be said of the 99%. We shared that experience. We were targeted as a country. Now, when it comes to this country's economic problems, we can't have shared sacrifice? That's the message of the Occupy Wall Street crowd. You know, the crowd that's calling themselves the 99%. Stop using us, abusing us, just respect us. Stop allowing greed and selfishness to be the only mantra of politicians and the 1%.

Here's a great solution. Let's start a new chapter in our lives. Let's evaluate our politicians by American standards. Any politician trying to restrict voting and change voting districts should be recalled and sent home. Any politician who thinks that only the 99% must pay for the economy with no contribution from the 1% should be recalled and sent home. Any politician who cannot at least respect the contribution of unions should be recalled and sent home. Now as all will notice, I mention recall a lot and that only applies to those 19 states who have the ability to recall state officials.[11] What did I just say? Many American, like myself, do not live in states that can recall state officials and that should change as soon as the next election. We must all pay attention or we will be repeating some of the more negative parts of our history. Another great solution for our unity is eliminating racial divisions. Stop believing the hype. Most White American have at least one Black or Hispanic friend. Okay, maybe an Asian friend also. Definitely a Jewish friend and most are just like you. We have lived here as long as you have and if you do not know minorities, that is on you. Minorities are an integral part of the 99%.

Just because we are the 99%, we can never accept the Republican agenda of not doing anything constructive. That agenda is blatantly anti-American and no one can pretend otherwise. President Obama has already been elected and this was our choice. To allow anyone to disrespect our choice is on us. To allow anyone to keep us unemployed, just to make our choice a one-term President, is on us. To keep allowing nothing getting accomplished just to keep us divided, is on us. We can not keep complaining when we elect people who cause chaos. We can not keep complaining when we elect those who tell us that we are not important because we are not the 1%. We are being treated like fools because we are unable to learn from history. I love the saying, "You break it, you own it." We have made this problem by not paying attention to our politicians and history. We have broken this country by not maintaining our majority. We have refused to do what we have to do to make it better, so, we own it. It's on us buddy, just because we are the 99%, it's on us.

It's the Economy, Stupid

On June 2001, President Bush approved a $1.35 trillion tax cut for the 1%.[1] On September 11, 2001, we were attacked. Then in 2003, President Bush enacted another tax cut and we were at war in two countries.[2] We went to war and never rescinded those tax cuts. Republicans stated that those tax cuts would not diminish revenue, they would increase revenue making the economy vibrant. They insisted that those tax cuts would not produce a deficit.[3] Unfortunately, they were incorrect. From 2005 to 2014, those tax cuts will add $2.8 trillion of direct cost and $1.1 trillion in interest payments resulting in adding $4 trillion to the deficit.[4] Where were the economic advisers? Did the lights go out and aliens took possession of the White House? What happened to reasoning? Since the Bush Administration never intended to pay for the two wars and the tax cuts were a freebie, there was little concern about the looming economic disaster. Therefore, we started President Obama's Administration with massive debt from unpaid wars, unpaid programs, and a screwed up housing and banking situation.[5] Just because the President is Barack Obama, those who made the economic disaster were allowed to shift the blame for the economic meltdown onto the President while they disrupted any type of recovery. The 99% bought the misinformation and accepted the disruptive behavior. Our continued economic disaster in 2011 was what the 2010 midterm elections contributed to our economy with our full support.

As long as the 99% refused to make those politicians, who were responsible for the financial meltdown, help in the cleanup, there would be no recovery in 2011. As long as the 99% allowed those politicians to remain in office, re-elected them, or did not recall them, there would be no recovery in 2011. Republicans promised jobs in 2010 with no intention of producing jobs in 20 anything, and they are all still in office. They are playing from the same playbook as George W. Bush so, we can expect no recovery in 2011 or maybe even 2012. Many of the 99% believed the President was at fault for not producing 14 million jobs in two years.[6] Those would be the jobs lost over the eight year period that George W. Bush was president. President Obama had two years of "NO" to everything, two years of constant bickering making as much chaos as possible, two years of Republicans dividing the 99%, and somehow, according to many of the 99%, the President was the problem. Really, is the 99% going to be played like that? Are we seriously that easy to con? I will perform my duty as a know-it-all and answer that question, yes, obviously we are.

We need to understand some basic economics. This should be the shortest chapter of all because this topic does not warrant a lot of discussion. However, I am a talker so let's just hope for the best. The 99% keeps looking to Washington and blaming the President for the lack of jobs. Job creation occurs in the states.[7] Let me say that again. Job creation occurs in the states. If you don't have a job, it is not President Obama fault, as FOX News would have you believe. It definitely is not because of the 2010 midterm U.S. Congress, who promised jobs and produced none. None of what I just said is the reason for lack of jobs. Yes, there have been policies that resulted in where we are right now. That would be the policies enacted by other administrations that gave businesses permission to take their jobs overseas, get corporate tax benefits, and deregulate their standards.[8] That would be policies that gave subsidies to corporations that did not need them.[9] That would be policies that occurred when we were not paying attention and living high off the economy. Even then, we were still being employed by the states. Times have changed, but the responsible parties have not and that would be the states.

The fact that 48 out of 50 states are in debt means that jobs will be scarce.[10] Sending differing opinions to Washington, as we did in the 2010 midterm elections, swearing that all we wanted was jobs and bipartisanship, was a big fat lie. Many of the 99% knew it was a lie but the desire for the President to fail was too enticing. However, none of those midterm voters seemed to connect the President's failing with the 99% failing with him. So, where we are, in 2011, is where voters decided we should be. Stop complaining about jobs or foreclosures or Medicare or anything because this was the decision of the 99%. Allowing those who made the problem back into office and allowing them to continue to work against the American people is 100% the fault of the 99%. Leave it to me to find the true culprits and I have done just that. The reason I can always identify the true culprit is because I am old and have lived a long time. I even have my Medicare card now so I really have a vested interest.

This is how the con began for the 2010 midterm shellacking. The glow that the 99% experienced, after electing the first African American into the presidency, was still on our cheeks when the misinformation began. Racists were furious at the election of an African American and joined the Republican party as Tea Party members. Okay, I'm kidding, they also joined the Democratic Party, but they felt more at home with Republicans. While the President believed that his election was the true American mandate of unifying the 99%, Republican faithfuls, FOX News, and all the other haters were working to confuse the 99%. Republicans refused to work to improve the economic meltdown they created with their deregulation and reckless behavior. They were working on the principle that their faithfuls would stay in line no matter how much they were being given the shaft, and they were correct. They just needed time to get the wishy-washy Independents back in line. So, Republicans went into overdrive with their negativity. They unified their message and hammered the 99% with a lot of misinformation. Their best outlet of misinformation was FOX News. If you heard one talking head on FOX News, you heard almost every talking head on FOX News, even down to the same phraseology. It worked as all mind control works. Luckily, thanks to Rupert Murdoch and the News of the World incident,[11] the entire world knows that Mr. Murdoch's FOX News is not a truthful institution. However, they fit right in with Republicans.

Republicans knew they could promise jobs and then not deliver. As of 2012, they have not delivered. They knew, if the voters put them back into office, they would be able to do absolutely anything to the 99% and that is exactly what they are doing. The midterm election of the party, who was responsible for jobs disappearing in the first place, was absolutely priceless. Somehow, the 99% thought their decision to return Republicans in massive amounts would work in their favor. To really make their point, the 99% elected a lot of Republicans everywhere, just so the President would get the message. Unfortunately, the 99% is now getting the real message in big print and they are paying the ultimate price with their choices. The midterm elections reinforced the 99% with their lazy, stupid, nothing status along with their racist status. Ha-ha-ha, oops, I mean I feel so bad. I didn't mean to start laughing yet. I have an entire book that I still have to write.

Let's allow this old woman to give the truth of the matter. Republicans were never going to produce jobs and those who elected them knew this fact. They have produced absolutely nothing, nada, zip, zero, zilch in 2011. They actually passed legislation that eliminated jobs.[12] Job creation is like family values for Republicans. These issues are just for campaigning because history has shown us that family programs are always the first programs that Republicans cut and unemployment rises with Republican Administrations.[13] They knew they didn't need to produce jobs and, as all can see, they are still not going to produce jobs. Job creation would not benefit them. It would benefit the 99% and the President. Republicans are not going to do that, not in this administration. They did not waste a year and a half of saying "NO" to everything to actually help the economy. All they had to do was just make the promise. This way many of the 99% could pretend, along with Republicans, that the issues were about jobs and not about race. Now, if what I just said is not true, then where are all of the dissenting voices to call out those newly elected Republicans who have made no effort to produce one job in 2011? Let's all be quiet for just a minute so we can hear those voices. Remember, this same now quiet dissenting crowd was quite vocal about electing more Republicans because they wanted more jobs and more bipartisanship. Jobs were not believable but bipartisanship was laughable. Republicans showed us that they would never, I repeat never, work with this President.[14] When representatives vote against their own bills, just to work against the President, bipartisanship will not ever happen.[15] However, I am still waiting to hear the multitude of dissenting voices on Republicans making no effort to produce any jobs (silence). Obviously, bipartisanship and job creation were never the agenda for those 2010 midterm voters. I guess none of those voters connected the desire by Republicans for the President to fail with their failing. I guess all of those voters had jobs and none of those voters were the 99%.

The 2010 midterm elections also produced more Republican governors because Republicans knew the key to the economy were the states. Those Republican governors started decimating their states and blaming the President. That particular tactic is the best of all. Think about it for a minute. States, who shifted their debt from one year to the next, are standing before their constituents telling them that their bad choices are some one else fault. How is President Obama responsible for state debt? Why are governors getting a free ride on job creation?

In 2011, we went back into the ditch. How much will the 99% connect what they did in 2010 with what is happening to them in 2011 and maybe 2012? Know-it-all me predicts the usual shifting the blame to Democrats and of course President Obama. I don't even have to wait this result out. This is exactly why we stay in the ditch because we are too divided and not aware of how our manipulated decisions affect everyone. For some crazy reason, we think only the President will be affected. Grow up America! We are all paying the price. I'm suppose to be working on my tan and here I am writing a book to explain the bad decisions that we keep making over and over again.

We are a foolish, fickle democracy but then lazy, stupid, nothings have been the demise of every democracy in history. Let's add this up for the 99% who want to pretend they can't figure this out. States are required by law to have a balanced budget.[16] Forty eight out of fifty states are in debt. That equals job losses. One solution for states would be more revenue like raising taxes on businesses and the wealthy. However, their only solution is taking down unions and state employees. Many businesses and corporations have move their jobs overseas. That equals job losses. One solution would be to eliminate tax breaks for overseas jobs which Congress has not done. So I ask again, why are so many of the 99% mad at President Obama and not the governors of their states, who are totally responsible for their joblessness, or Congress who will not remove the tax breaks? Tea Party, Oh Tea Party, I have an anger issue for you. Where are your voices? I will repeat myself because I know that the Tea Party did not hear me the first time. Job losses are because of STATES not the President. The President has written and submitted a jobs bill. Congress has refused to pass that jobs bill. This would be the jobs bill that technically Congress is responsible for writing since that was their 2010 promise and their Constitutional responsibility. However, what does it really matter because the states governed by Republican governors will either send the jobs bill money back to the Federal Government or find a way to use it to balance their budgets.[17] Despite the Republican's promised platform of job creation, to date, President Obama's agenda is the only plan that is slowly producing jobs. Did I explain that simple enough for everyone?

If it's the economy, then everyone should be working to improve the economy. That is not hard to understand. We must never allow any opposing party to work against the economy. Republicans are on record for "NO" on everything. They were against helping any business that was failing, especially the auto companies. All of the companies, including the auto companies, are paying the government back their loans. They are on record for being against extended unemployment. That's right, they are against the 99% getting the unemployment benefits that they, their employers, or both paid into when the 99% was working. Go figure! According to Republicans, those who are unemployed do not want jobs because they are okay getting government money or just plain lazy, drug addicted, breeding hobos.[18] Wow! That is harsh and I know that was intended for people like the 99% who are occupying Wall Street. Okay yes, I did call the 99% lazy, stupid, nothings but that is not as harsh as that drug addicted hobo part. However, now that I think about it, putting Republicans back in office does make me think of some type of drug addiction.

Republicans were all for allowing the country to bankrupt. They promised absolutely nothing, and they were elected into office in 2010. Oh, that's right, they did promise one thing. They promised jobs with no intention of producing those jobs because jobs would have benefited the President.[19] If it's the economy, those who refuse to make any effort to improve that economy, Republicans, must be sent home. Those who voted against job bills, Republicans, must be sent home.[20] Those who voted against eliminating subsidies for big businesses, Republicans, must be sent home.[21] Those who have not even made an effort at any type of jobs bill, Republicans, must be sent home. I know, I know, Republicans will convince their base that they will produce jobs <u>after</u> President Obama is defeated. Why not, right? If their base bought the jobs creation in 2010, they certainly can wait two lousy years for the possibility of jobs creation in 2013. There are plenty of homeless shelters in the United States, it's only two lousy years. There must be some available tents in the park with the Occupy Wall Street groups (giggles). So America, just wait. The culprits who made the problem will solve all your problems and unemployment, just like they promised they would before the 2010 midterm elections. It will just be two years late. Or maybe, just maybe, we are starting the era of the really really rich and the really really poor. Whatever, we bought the cow and now we have no milk. What? Sorry, I was looking at a milk commercial.

Just because we are the 99%, we decided to elect chaos. We tied the President's hands and then complained that he caves on everything. We placed him in enemy territory and then were angry because he could not get us out of danger. We stacked the deck with nothing but Jokers. You need to play cards to understand that one. We made the monster and now we want to pretend that our hands are clean. Listen, I have a million of these sayings. Well, as long as I am old, black, and a woman, I will continue to remind everyone of our lazy, stupid, nothingness and I will always place the blame for our present and our future on us, the 99%. We chose to elect chaos and we got chaos. There is no sense in complaining because we are the majority of voters, you know, the 99%. We have kicked our own butt because of the way we have allowed ourselves and the economy to be manipulated. The only solutions to our economy are jobs and shared sacrificing. It will always be the economy, because money is the only driving force in the world. It's just the economy, stupid, and the 99% is the loser by its own hands.

JOBS, WHAT JOBS?

The 99% made a bold decision in November 2010. They decided to trust Republicans again. That would be the very same Republicans who lost jobs for eight years.[1] Now, looking at that move on paper, it looked like a stupid move. Actually, there is no way that you could look at that move without it being a stupid move, but what do I know? That statement of "What do I know" was rhetorical because I am a know-it-all and proud of that. Anyway, voters decided to stop forward progress and go with Republicans, real time job producers (giggles).

When Republicans promised jobs in the 2010 midterm elections, many of the 99% thought that it was a good idea. The fact that those same individuals worked against the country for a year and a half was a moot point. The only thing that mattered was that Republicans promised jobs. So, since no one wanted to wait on President Obama's slow and steady progress of economic stability, the 99% decided to go with the speedy, we can produce jobs right away, Republicans. It was totally believable because of their record of such high job creation. NOT! Let me think for just a moment to see if I can recall when that occurred. The last Republican president lost jobs in his administration. I am sure that there must have been a day when jobs were created but I can't come up with it right now. However, that is not relevant since many of the 99% have already made the decision to go with the Republican agenda of producing jobs. Ignore their talk about reducing government because I am sure there would be no job losses. NOT! Ignore that crazy talk about getting rid of Medicare because I am really sure there would be no job losses. NOT! Ignore all of that spending cuts crap because reduction of programs does not always mean job reduction. NOT! Ha-ha, I absolutely must prepare my Everglades property for the 99% because I truly have some big fish on my line.

I finished this book at the beginning of 2012. Where are the Republican jobs? I waited patiently, all of 2011, for those jobs that Republicans promised. The 99% hit the streets and still no jobs. While the President was still slowly stabilizing the economy which was making it easier for states and companies to produce jobs, the jobs promising Republicans gave us nothing, not even a bill. I went about my daily life and knew that if no jobs were produced, the masses would rise up and expel those miscreants. (I'm reading a little Shakespeare, while I'm waiting, and that's why miscreants came into the conversation.) It's just another way of saying evildoer, villainous or anyone who behaves badly (giggles). Anyway, I am still waiting because the "We are the only ones who can produce jobs" Republicans have not produced anything. What Republicans have done instead is enacted polices that have already cost 500,000 public sector jobs in 50 states.[3] So, of course, I am a little confused because there has been no massive screaming and blaming Republicans. Yes, the 99% is occupying Wall Street but no one is targeting Republicans and asking where are their jobs. Where is all the outrage at the promise of jobs and no effort to create jobs? President Obama came into office with the worst economic disaster ever and still he was able to gradually start creating incentives for job creating initiatives through his stimulus and his policies. However, the impatient public decided to abandon ship. There has been no outcry of "Get rid of those lying Republicans." There has been no outcry of "They lied to us and manipulated our subconscious and conscious racism." Though, I do understand why no one wants to admit to that second one, very un-American. Where are all of those who complained so bitterly before the 2010 midterm elections and, get this, are now staying very quiet? Instead, the 99% is still blaming President Obama and asking "Where are the jobs?" Wow, this is so embarrassing. The 99% usually tries to cover its racism better than this but, I guess, desperate times call for desperate measures.

After a year and a ten months, we changed parties to those who will not and can not produce anything. Those same miscreants still continue to convince the 99% to blame the President, who took a shellacking in the 2010 midterm elections, about what else, jobs. Okay sidebar, I know everyone noticed my will not and can not remark. Republicans will not produce jobs because they have voted "NO" on any jobs bill that has been submitted.[4] An improved economy benefits President Obama. Remember, according to Republicans, President Obama is going to be a one-term President. So, Republicans will not help the 99% because that is not their agenda. Republicans can not produce jobs because they have to help the 1% and that means that everything must be cut from the 99% so that those who have 85% of the wealth can get the remaining 15%.[5] Sorry about that 99%, you got conned again.

Now, I know conservatives will say that I am just being a silly old liberal and not telling the truth. I say yes to old, yes to liberal, but never to silly, but definitely the truth. Anyway, at this point, conservatives can not say a thing about anyone being silly because they continue to back a party, Republicans, who tell them that they are a distant second to the 1%. As I so eloquently said before, the 30% of you who support the Republican party are not the 1%. An important detail to take note. Your 30% falls right in there with the rest of the 99%. When your Republicans cut programs that benefit the 99% to keep tax cuts and subsidies for the 1%, you are affected just like the rest of the 99%.

In the first five months of 2011, there were no jobs or jobs bill produced by Republicans. Instead of creating jobs, Republicans in the House repealed Obama's healthcare on behalf of the health insurance industry. Then they voted to end Medicare so they could protect Big Oil giveaways.[6] Then they decided to go after the Environmental Protection Agency (EPA), to help the big polluters, of course. Tell me 99%, just from those three initiatives that I just mentioned, do you feel that Republicans are looking out for your best interest? Do you see any job creation from those initiatives? They voted to allow corporations, shipping jobs overseas, to keep their tax breaks. They voted to allow corporations and any special interest to donate to presidential campaigns, without any disclosure or consequences, so that they could continue to lie to you. They voted to stop funding public radio stations and Planned Parenthood.[7] Does any of this sound like job creation yet? Republicans voted for bills that would stall any economic recovery because they do not care about producing jobs. They voted to undermine education, infrastructure, college aid, research, and of course clean energy. As far as I can tell, none of these initiatives produced any jobs. As a matter of fact, these initiative could result in the loss of millions of jobs.[8]

Democrats in the House have tried to pass bills that will produce high skill, high paying jobs. The only job bills that Republicans have voted on has been Democratic bills and they voted to kill those bills. Please remember again, Republicans shellacked the President because of jobs, or so everyone would like to tell us. Yet, here we are, in 2012, with no jobs created by Republicans. They voted against, not for, a bill that would stop government contracts being awarded to corporations who are shipping our jobs overseas. They voted against, not for, investing in our economy by rebuilding our schools, our hospitals, and transportation infrastructure.[8]

I know that Governor Rick Scott of Florida declined a High Speed Rails program which would have created hundreds of jobs. Governor Scott is my governor and I do not particularly like him. The reason is because his company defrauded Medicare and it is difficult for me to trust someone after that antic. I like to quote George W. Bush "Fool me once, shame on—shame on you, fool me—you can't get fooled again (giggles). I miss the wit of Bush II. President Obama is too cool to look that idiotic, but I try to understand those who thought Bush II was intelligent. NOT! Anyway, where was I? They voted against, not for, American Job Act, Manufacturing Strategy Act, Vehicle Manufacturing Technology Act, and the Fair Trade Act.[9] All of those bills could have produce millions of jobs but since this Republican Congress is not about job creation, they were required to vote "NO." Even I am tired of the constant "NO" to everything that is good for the 99%. Why, may I ask, isn't the 99% tired of this childish and reckless behavior? Even more importantly, where are all of those who were so outraged because the President did not produce jobs fast enough? Republicans did not have an economic disaster impeding their job creation so why is there no outrage at Republicans who, as all can see, have no intention of producing any jobs. This sure looks racial to me because if this was really about job creation then the 99% would be on the street bitching and complaining. I certainly hope that is what the Occupy Wall Street 99% is marching and getting arrested for. Better still, the 99% should be recalling as I am typing this section. Where are you 99%? I don't see you anywhere and I am still typing (giggles).

The only solution Republicans have for our economy is to return to their old failed policies that do not create jobs. Those failed policies of tax cuts and deregulation were responsible for our financial meltdown. Those policies continue to give every tax break on the planet to the wealthy and corporations. Since these old failed policies have always been the Republican agenda and there is no true intention of creating jobs, Congress stays on vacation. The House, who started in January 2011, has been vacationing in the months of February, April, May, August, November, and December.[10] I know the House does not intend to do anything but can't they at least pretend? It amazes me that Republicans do not care how the 99% sees their actions. I guess they know that this is not about logic, just about race because they have their solid 30%. Watching that 30% being maneuver by the Tea Party and watching them pretend they are okay with their treatment is a joy to watch. Make no bones about it, I will continue to laugh at the 30% who are caught in their own web. I will be laughing so hard I will fall off my chair, tears will run down my cheeks, my nose will start running, and I will pass out from glee. I have informed my family of what will happen so that they will not call an ambulance. I have health insurance so I can afford the ambulance, if necessary (giggles).

After eight months of Republicans not creating any initiatives to produce more jobs and with them still placing the blame on President Obama, the President decided to perform the job of Congress. He gave the American people a jobs bill.[11] Now, let me quickly show everyone my Constitutional knowledge. According to the Constitution, which Republicans swear they are following to the letter, Congress and Congress alone is responsible for making bills. There is no shared responsibility. Yes, the President can present his ideas to congressional members and they can write his bill. The House or the Senate enacts the bill and the President only has the capacity to pass the bill or veto the bill. Now, does everyone understand everyone's role? This theory also works with job creation. The President and Congress do not create jobs. Congress can write bills to make job creation easier for companies and the President can pass or veto that bill, but governors and the states are the job creators. When local municipalities lose jobs because companies move away, the states lose jobs.[12] When the state legislature does not send enough money for education and healthcare, the local municipalities lose jobs and the states lose more jobs. The President nor Congress have anything to do with states losing jobs. Governors, however, do have everything to do with states losing jobs, if you just have to blame someone. Now once again, does everyone understand everyone's role. If 48 our of 50 states are in debt and have to lay off workers, how does this rest solely on the President's shoulders? States did not just go into debt in 2009, no way. States have been in debt for some time.

So now that we understand what I thought was so obvious, why were the President's numbers suffering in 2010 and 2011? Why, in this entire country of responsible people, is the blame being placed solely on the President's shoulders? Did we forget, 99%, that we flooded Congress and states with job promising Republicans? There are only two million Federal employees. The remaining 150 million or more workers are with states or private companies in those states.[13] As a matter of fact, a few of the Republican candidates for the presidency were governors and they all claimed job creation. There claims were always the number of jobs they created in their state and they were absolutely correct.[14] Why? Because job creation is in the states not the President's office. Can regulations and standards help with job creation? Of course! However, that is on Congress. Does everyone understand the words coming out of my mouth? My point is that no one was blaming Bush II for the growing unemployment. No one was blaming Bush II for the dismal economic conditions. No one had anything to say until the black man showed up and then everything on the planet became his fault. That is definitely true of FOX News. My goodness, they are so racist it is almost painful to watch. That, plus the fact that they manipulate the news, is the reason I do not watch FOX News. You cannot trust people who lie like that.

Republicans only talking points are that the President has not produced jobs. Ignore the fact that governors are let off the hook for job creation. Ignore the fact that Republicans campaigned on job creation and so far have produced none. We all feel that the unemployment rate is too high. If the Federal Government tries to send money to states as a stimulus, governors either turn it down or hide it in their budgets. You know the old tactic of paying for the debt ridden expenditures that occurred before this President and covering those same expenditures with Federal money calling it their budget instead of stimulus money.[15] After all, didn't Republicans convince the 99% that the stimulus did not help them with one job. I know about this hiding the stimulus because Governor Scott of Florida turned down money for High Speed Rails and then quietly hid Federal stimulus money in his budget.[16] States are suppose to balance their budgets but most are in debt. Why are governors let off the hook even while they try to balance their budgets on the backs of the 99%? This sure looks like a "Just because the President is black" reason to me, which always results in a "Just because we are the 99%" outcome.

As I said before, Congress was not passing anything, so the President jumped into the fray. The President challenged the Congress to pass his jobs bill, NOW. That request was made September 7, 2011. At the publishing of this book in February 2012, Congress had not passed his bill. So 99%, since you voted for this do nothing Congress, who is responsible for the lack of jobs? You hammered the President, putting all of the responsibility of job production on him, and he responded with a jobs bill. Congress did nothing with that jobs bill or any other Democratic jobs bill and still the 99% sits and blames the President and Congress equally. Why the equal blame? If the 99% wants to use any excuse to replace the President, stop hiding the true reason for wanting him gone and change administrations. Just remember however, actions have consequences. The 99% made the 2010 decision with its eyes wide open and that action produced chaos. We waited in 2011 and the consequences were no jobs. Are we to assume that Republicans will produce jobs in 2012? NOT!

According to a September 2011 poll, Independents believed Republicans were better at producing jobs than the President, 44% to 32%.[17] By October 2011, because of the President's Jobs Bill, Independents believed the President was better at producing jobs than Republicans. Here is my question. Why were Independents still thinking that Republicans were better at job creation when there had been no attempt by Republicans to create jobs from midterm 2010 until September 2011? What's the criteria that Independents were using to justify their belief in who was creating jobs? Now, everyone can understand why I keep referring to Independents as wishy washy. Before the midterm elections, we were creating jobs through the President's policies and initiatives and then Independents and others of the 99% decided to hogtie the President with more of the party of "NO." As if the election did not even occur, voters still felt the President was responsible. Remember Independents and other voters of the 2010 midterm elections, you rejected the President's methods because you were told that the country was going in the wrong direction. From midterm 2010 to 2012, this would be on you, the voters who made the decision to change our progress. Your wishy washy behavior is on you and your fellow voters. Take it like the manipulated targets that you are.

Isn't everyone tired of the mistreatment by those elected into office? Isn't everyone ashamed of the way they have allowed the 1% to manipulate the 99%? Big corporation do not care at all. I know everyone has heard that Walmart is going to require their full-time employees to pay more into their health insurance and part-time employees will not have any coverage at all.[18] The 1% is really socking it to the 99%. Here we have a giant corporation, making billions, wanting their minimum wage workers to share in the rise in healthcare. Isn't that special. You have to love greed because it is never ending. The 1% and Republicans do not want to share in helping the country out of this recession. They want to make sure that the 99% does not ever recover. The workers of Walmart will have to either absorb the cost, have no healthcare, or quit. With 14 million or more of the 99% unemployed, they certainly will not quit. Walmart also had a discriminatory policy against women as was evident by the class action suit lodged against them. Our middle class hating Supreme Court dismissed this lawsuit in favor of expensive one lawyer/one client lawsuits which would drastically eliminate most of those who were in the original lawsuit.[19] Walmart is almost as bad as Bank of American who tried to add an ATM fee on our debit cards. Hey, 99%, we need to take this non caring attitude. Let's all just quit our jobs and see how quickly the 1% falls apart. Ha-ha, I was just kidding because they know they have us over a barrel. We need jobs to exist and, unfortunately, they can wait us out. What we can do instead is go back to small businesses. We can shop at small local markets and bank at small banks and credit unions.[20] We can make changes that let those big greedy corporations understand that they can not disrespect us. Well, it was just a thought. The problem of jobs will take a long time because we refuse to unify for our own good. We refuse to really be the 99%. As long as we blame the President, any president, for what our states are responsible for and what we voted for, we keep giving the 1% our power.

Just because we are the 99%, we can make "Made in America" our job creation. We need to manufacture our way out of this job problem. Diane Sawyer of ABC News showed a program about a builder and his "Made in America" house. He used no foreign products. He made a list and many people were ecstatic about bringing products, materials, and possible manufacturing opportunities back to the states. Ironically, when Lowe's and Home Depot were approached about carrying those "Made in America" products, Lowe's stated it would special order and Home Depot stated if enough people ordered the products they would start carrying those products.[21] Are you kidding me? These two giants do not normally carry all American products in America. I will bet you that the Chinese can get any and all Chinese made products in China. Is this where we are at this time in our history? The 99% having to hunt for "Made in America" products? Let's change that. I need for some computer geek to set up a site that tells the 99% what percentage of the products on our shelves are bought by the 99%. If we buy 50% of that product, then 50% of the manufacture jobs of that product should be here in the United States. If the company does not want to move factories then we must stop buying that product. If a company or corporation does not care whether we have money to buy their product, then we do not need to purchase their product. This is the premises behind "Made in America." If a company does not want to manufacture in America, then we can not keep buying their product. Recently, Whirlpool bought Maytag and then fired everyone in the United States.[22] Therefore, the 99% must say goodbye to Whirlpool and Maytag products. No one is saying that a corporation can't have factories elsewhere but they can not completely deplete us of a way to make a living just because they are greedy. This can become our new movement. This is what the various "Occupy . . ." protestors are saying in their demonstrations. "Made in America" must become our new mantra and maybe the 99% can stop asking, jobs, what jobs.

LEGISLATORS FROM HELL

When the President took a shellacking about jobs in the 2010 midterm elections, the legislators from hell were placed into office. According to the 99%, our economy had not improved significantly in one year and ten months. The 99% decided to believe Republicans. I guess one would have to assume that the 99% felt Republican's past performance of a financial meltdown and rising unemployment was not an indicator of their future behavior of producing jobs. I guess the 99% decided not to learn from history. Why would unions back the Republican Party who hates unions and has said so for years? Why would women vote for this party who wants government out of their lives but not out of their vagina? What convinced teachers that their jobs would be safe when this party has stated that they wanted education privatized and teacher's tenures eliminated? Republicans showed everyone their desire to eliminate regulations even those that were beneficial to the 99%. Republican legislator's record and rhetoric told their true agenda of reduced taxes for the rich, increased corporate tax deductions, and union busting, but the President was black and the 99% was divided. Republicans, with the help of FOX News, convinced the public to follow them blindly because the President was black and the 99% was divided. The 99% believed the campaign to misinform them about President Barack Obama. The 99% did not listen to or believe the Republican divisive rhetoric. With that mindset, the 99% elected the legislators from hell. Those legislators showed the 99% the true Republican's mandate which was anti-big government, taxes, unions, abortion, healthcare reform, infrastructure development, gay rights, social welfare, immigration, compromise, any program for the less fortunate, and any policy or initiative from President Obama.

The first legislator who came to the spotlight was Governor Scott Walker of Wisconsin. I laughed, in my first book, at Wisconsin residents because they had a nice little government that worked for them. They allowed misinformation to change the landscape. Actually, the people said they were frustrated by unemployment, the housing crisis, and all of the struggles of the economy which Republicans blamed on the President and promised they would do better. Ignoring history, the people of Wisconsin bought the rhetoric and elected a Republican governor and a Republican legislature. Wisconsinites did not do their homework. Governor Walker was not born two hours before he ran for office, he had a paper trail. Governor Walker's anti-union attitudes went back to when he was on the Milwaukee Country Board of Supervisors.[1] Governor Walker started his administration with his controversial policy to strip teachers, nurses, and other public employees of most of their collective bargaining rights.[2] His budget also proposed huge cuts to education, seniors, and healthcare. This governor and other Republican governors recent actions are clever maneuvers to eliminate the political power of unions. No matter how much the people of Wisconsin are complaining now, they brought this particular brand of chaotic mess on themselves and they are in the fight of their lives.

According to the Wisconsin Legislative Fiscal Bureau, Governor Walker entered office with a surplus of $121 million.[3] Wow! That's like President George W. Bush who entered office with a $300 billion surplus. Governor Walker immediately gave millions to corporations as subsidies and then proclaimed the need to cut spending because of his man-made deficit. Wow! That's the same as President George W. Bush who immediately gave tax cuts and subsidies upon entering into office and ended with a huge deficit. Governor Walker instigated this deficit so that he could target unions.[3] He targeted collective bargaining, despite the fact that cutting collective bargaining did not balance the budget. This was the one non-negotiable item on the Governor's agenda. The people protested but the Governor and his legislature rammed the union busting bill through. Now, the people of Wisconsin realize that they might have been duped. They might have elected a little dictator. Governor Walker is propped up by the Kock Brothers, who were the Governor's second largest contributors and who have an anti-union agenda. The Kock Brothers have several energy companies, like coal subsidiaries, timber plants, and a large network of pipelines. There is a provision in the Governor's budget repair bill that allows the state to sell or contract out any state-owned energy assets in no-bid deals.[1] Wonder who will get those no-bid, state-owned, contracts? Anyone want to guess? The dishonesty just never ends. Hold on, wait minute! Aren't the Kock Brothers the same people funding the famous Tea Party?[4] The Tea Party was suppose to be the angry common man or 99% until the real 99% showed up on Wall Street. The 1% loves to use the common man for their nefarious purposes (giggles).

Protestors and especially teachers objected to the Governor's union busting agenda. Governor Walker felt he needed an ally to legitimize his misinformation. Naturally, FOX News jumped into the fray and tried to convince the people of Wisconsin that their teachers were overpaid and actually wealthy. Bill O'Reilly, of The O'Reilly Factor, even had the audacity to say that teacher's salaries and benefits were "lavish."[5] Seriously, who would listen to a talking head, who gets paid millions, sitting for an hour a day, as opposed to a teacher and their very long day with a room full of children? After the Governor's assault on teachers, the next agenda was the state employee pension fund, which was 99% funded and one of the healthiest in the nation.[6] Governor Walker and his right-wing accomplices misinformed and manipulated the people of Wisconsin. What makes this so uniquely funny is that Wisconsinites believed the misinformation about President Obama and Democrats being the only responsible parties in our economic meltdown. Those lies help them to elect many Republican representatives never realizing that they would become targets also. I love that old saying, "What goes around, comes around." Sorry, I have to admit that was crass of me (giggles).

Now, the question has to be how will the people of Wisconsin get themselves out of this quicksand? I must say "Bravo" to the people of Wisconsin for trying to recall some of their legislators especially since the 99% does not recall that much.[7] We seem to take the "Grin and bear it" mantra to heart. However, millions of dollars flowed into Wisconsin during the recall because the wealthy always have their middle class henchmen.[8] The recall of the legislators did not produce the desired results but it helped elected officials understand that Wisconsin voters are going to keep fighting, which is all they can do at this point. Wisconsinites are still trying to rectify their mistake and have issued a petition for the recall of the Governor. Way to go Wisconsinites, but watch your back. There are always those who think they will gain something from the chaos or maybe just because the President is black, who knows and who cares because Wisconsinites brought this mess on themselves. They did not do their homework. Well really, they did not read my first book, which would have saved them. Ha-ha, good luck Wisconsin.

The next legislator is Governor Rick Synder from Michigan. Governor Synder is going one step farther than Governor Walker. Not only does he want collective bargaining rights and taxes on pensions, he also wants to prohibit strikes by certain public employees.[9] However, the most sinister of all of his policies is his Financial Marshall Law.[10] He is proposing to take control of local municipalities with Emergency Managers, from his administration, and rejecting duly elected officials of those local municipalities. Can anyone spell dictatorship? Selecting and electing our own representatives is a democratic right. Granted, we do a lousy job but it's still our right. However, with this bunch of Republicans, we cannot afford to lose any of our rights. Dictatorships are formed with Emergency managers from the administrations in charge. How will this end for Michigan voters or will this law just eliminate the voter part in government? Apparently, according to Governor Synder, voters do not matter. Who knows how this will end. Like I said, the people of Michigan bought the con and now they, like the people of Wisconsin, must fight for their rights all over again. I have to laugh, just a little, because it is unbelievable that so many of the 99% drank the Kool-Aid. (Jim Jones reference, look it up.) Republicans made the economic disaster and thanks to their fellow henchmen, FOX News, they convinced many of the 99% to drink the Kool-Aid willingly (giggles). Black Americans had to march for their rights in this country. It will be fascinating to see how the 99% will fight for their rights. You can borrow our "We shall overcome" song. Oops, too late, Gay Americans already have our song. Well, it's okay because we all share for the cause.

The next legislator is Governor Rick Scott of my home state of Florida. I am laughing really hard at the residents of Florida because this Governor showed Floridians exactly what he was about before he was elected. When asked why his company was fined over a billion dollars in Medicare fraud, of which he claimed to have no knowledge, his only answer was that he would not talk about it.[11] Floridians let him get away with no explanation just because of their rush to punish the President. Floridians are already teased about the hanging chads incident. Now this Governor, whose only claim to fame was Medicare fraud, getting elected in a state full of senior citizens is priceless. Poor Florida senior citizens, this is so embarrassing. Hey, wait a minute! I am a Florida senior citizen. However, I did not vote for this Governor. I am among the few senior citizens holding up our generation and it is tedious, but I must make my grands proud.

Here is the gist of the matter. If Rick Scott was not aware of massive fraud in his own medical company, how would he handle a state? What kind of CEO is not aware when his company is defrauding the government? Isn't that fraud an example of Rick Scott's inability to lead? Well, right out of the gate, Governor Scott decided to drug test every state employee and Medicaid recipients. That's right, Medicaid recipients, because you have to go with what you know. One of Solantic, an urgent care chain co-founded by Governor Rick Scott, more popular services is, you guessed it, drug testing. When it was brought to the Governor's attention, that this sudden drug testing was suspicious and Solantic was owned by him, he moved his holdings to a trust in, you guessed it, his wife's name. Nothing suspicious about that, right? Then the Governor tried to push Medicaid into private HMO's because Solantic, you guessed it, does not accept Medicaid, only private HMO's.[12] I never thought that the Governor would jump right back into medical issues so quickly after being elected, but you know the old saying, time is money. I guess Governor Scott is back into medical fraud mode but who can blame him? He profited so well the first time. However, Republicans will stand tall with this Governor because admitting that they have been conned, duped, and made a fool of is not something they can admit. Make no bones about it, I am laughing at all of those who bought the con and all of those who knew they were being conned but too ashamed to admit their idiocy. I absolutely love it.

Unfortunately, there is more for Floridians. According to AARP issue, October 2011, the Governor and the legislature slashed $188 million from Medicaid nursing home funding and reduced staffing standards. According to Politics Nation on December 28, the Governor and the legislature have also rejected $37 million for disabled senior citizens, $2 million for Medicare Outreach, and $1 million for the Health Care Exchange. Approximately 21% of Floridians are without health insurance, which is the third highest rate in the country, and yet Governor Rick Scott is declining help for those 21%. Wow! It is really going to suck being a senior citizen or anyone without health insurance in Florida. Anyway, Governor Scott's ratings are very low and maybe Floridians will get some balls and recall. If there are any questions, just ask the people of Miami-Dade, Florida, because we know how to recall.[13] Wait a minute! Florida is not a state that can recall state officials. So, Floridians are just plain stuck with what they elected into office. I guess it is safe to assume that I am not an admirer of Governor Scott and it is not personal. It's just not wise to place a person who has been involved in fraudulent activity in government where fraudulent activity is so prevalent. It's like giving a thief the keys to the vault. I am all about second chances but since there was no penalty for the first fraudulent activity, there is no incentive to not commit more fraudulent activity.

The next legislator is hard talking Governor Chris Christie of New Jersey. Republicans were really desperate for this Governor to be their Republican candidate in the 2012 race for the White House. Governor Christie decided not to be their scapegoat but it looks as if he might be interested in the vice presidency. Go figure! He should know the Republican party is a disaster. If Republicans one and only favorite, President Reagan, could not pass the acid test for most strict right-wing conservatives, Governor Christie knew he would not meet their requirements for getting the Republican nomination. He's trying to wait the zealots out. Good luck! He decided instead to stay and torture the people of New Jersey. His claim to fame is his attempt to privatize New Jersey public schools.[14] He wanted private companies to operate and improve 200 of New Jersey's chronically failing schools. Republicans have been pushing privatization for quite some time and what it really boils down to is allowing their buddies, corporations, and private companies to get some of that education money. Big, old, bad Federal Government sends money to states for education and why waste it on improving schools when private companies can make a bigger profit for themselves?[15] If there are only 200 chronically failing schools in New Jersey, then there must be at least 200 schools that are succeeding. Rather than striping schools, duplicate what works in "A" schools. The money that private companies will profit off of education would more than pay for the improvement of those failing schools. Instead, Governor Christie would rather propose cuts to school spending and then complain about failing schools. Does everyone see how this con works? This is why we really, really must pay attention to those we place in office because there are a lot of underhanded maneuvers that we are not aware of but end up paying for over and over again.

Governor Christie also announced his intention to withdraw from the Regional Greenhouse Gas Initiative.[16] This initiative is a multi-state climate and energy program to reduce energy cost, reduce air pollution from fossil fuels, and stimulate the clean energy economy. This program has contributed to reduced emissions from power plants, as well as increases in energy efficiency, job creation, and economic growth in other states. This sounds like a great program for the humans of earth. So why would anyone not want this initiative? However, this rejection should not come as a shock to anyone because Republicans refuse to believe in scientific facts about global warming. Republicans are consistent about never allowing facts to enter into any of their thinking. It is all about money, money, and who will make more money.

The next legislator is Governor Nathan Deal of Georgia. Governor Deal passed a strict immigration bill and illegals fled from the state.[17] Great, that's what Georgia residents wanted, right? Now there will be more jobs for the residents of Georgia. Unfortunately, those are the jobs that the 99% does not appear to want. No matter what we feel about immigration, immigrants, legal or illegal, are the people picking our crops. As a result of this immigration bill, the crops started rotting on the vines because Georgians had no intention of sweating in the fields, like black slaves. The Governor decided that he would use criminals to pick the crops and the criminals said there was no way they were going to work that hard. No way, Jose! He also decided to use those same criminals as firefighters because its cheaper. I hope the residents of Georgia understand the use of criminals so that the wealthy can keep their taxes, but it might be a good idea to at least eliminate arsonist from the criminal fire force (giggles). Sometimes, it pays to think a problem through first and then enact the bill. However, hatred for illegal immigrants, especially Hispanic immigrants, overruled common sense and Republicans did what they do best and showed their ignorance and unconcern for their fellow man. Apparently, there was a little hatred for firefighters also. Who knew? After this immigration bill fiasco, guess who else decided to implement the same type of bill? Yes, that would be the state of Alabama.[18] Their farmers are just as pissed about their crops rotting in the field as the Georgia farmers. I would have thought that just living in either of those states would be pissy enough. Okay, I live in Florida and I have a dud of a governor and legislature also, so I can not talk, but I can laugh. Since southern states like to look stupid as a unit, Mississippi decided to go everyone better with their abortion bill.[19] They had a bill which was a shoo-in to pass because Mississippians are staunchly conservative. That bill would have declared a blood clot as a human being. At the moment of conception, that clot would have had the same rights as a 90 year old man. There would have been no requirement of the clot being able to breathe on its own which might have been tricky since one of the requirements of death is not being able to breath on ones own. Well, the south will rise again with this thinking and it will sink just as fast because it has a bevy of crazy representatives duly elected. Mississippians, however, rejected this crazy bill so there is hope for the south once again.

Another Republican legislator is Ohio Governor John Kasich who, like all the other Republican governors, also targeted unions. He verbally attacked a police officer and called him an idiot when he was ticketed for not yielding to an emergency vehicle on the side of the road.[20] Apparently, the Governor felt he did not have to abide by the law. I guess he wanted police unions and other state employee unions mad at him as a unit. My favorite action by Governor Kasich is his declaration making the Dallas Mavericks basketball team honorary Ohioans when they beat Miami in the finals.[21] I told everyone in my last book to stop the hating and apparently I must send the same message again. Get over it, Governor! LeBron James is on my Miami Heat team and he is happy. He will probably be a Heat player longer than you will be governor but nobody really cares. Man up, Governor, and move on! Do serious stuff like trying to get your Senate Bill 5 (S.B.5) passed. You know which bill I'm talking about. S.B.5 limits bargaining abilities of 350,000 teachers, nurses, firefighters, police, and other public workers. It bans strikes, scraps binding arbitration, and eliminates teacher's step increases.[22] Way to go Governor Kasich, alienate all of the voters in your state. Anyway, the public fought back and in November they voted against S.B.5.[23] Hooray! Is the next step recall of the Governor?

Then there is legislator Mitch Daniels, Governor of Indiana, who was Bush II's economic adviser.[24] Come on Indiana, you had to know that this Governor was not going to be in your corner. Governor Daniels immediately rescinded the collective bargaining rights of state workers.[25] He is trying to convert his state to a "Right to work" state which would create lots of low paying jobs for the 99%. Republicans were desperate for this Governor to run for the presidency also. The remaining Republican governors are anywhere from Alaska to South Carolina and they all have the same agenda and pretended mandate with the results of the 1% keeping their wealth, the 99% losing their programs, and unions being decimated hopefully weakening the Democratic party. So 99%, keep up the good work. Keep believing in those who keep showing you their butt just because the President is Barack Obama. Keep allowing them to con you to the wazoo. Keep dividing your 99% and ignore the laughter that you hear. Some of it will be me but the roar of laughter will be from the Republican Party and the controlling 1%. Job well done, guys.

Most Republican governors and their legislatures are also trying to redraw their legislative districts so that they keep control.[26] Since this has been a work in progress, they have accomplished some of their agenda which is silent control of the votes to implement the squashing of the 99%. If most of our districts are Republican districts and Republicans have no concern about their manipulation, then the agenda of the 1% becomes the American agenda. That agenda is the 1% controls everything and the 99% gets nothing. Yep, that seems about right to me if you listen to the Republican's rhetoric. This is not the way a democracy is suppose to operate, and here the 99% thought they had a real democracy. Silly 99%!

As a southerner, my favorite legislators from hell are those from the south. Governors from the south are consistent in their dislike for this President and they love being junior Republicans. The Old South, of discriminatory fame, keeps trying to rise again. For some reason, the South just cannot escape their craziness. Probably, this is because they can not let go of the issue of race. Their continued tributes to old racist flags, confederate leaders, and separatist documents is getting embarrassing.[27] They can not move on because for some reason they are stuck. No matter how many steps forward the South takes, they keep allowing their crazies to come back to the surface and destroy all forward progress. Years and years of this constant need to celebrate the old South and segregation is really embarrassing. This is the reason no one likes to take the South seriously. Come on South! Move on! Get a grip and come into this century. There is absolutely no reason to completely come apart at the seams just because the President is black. You knew it would happen sometimes. Well, maybe not because I sure was shocked and I am a know-it-all. However I can move on and be shocked sitting on a beach in Florida.

Along with the governors from hell, the 99% elected a ton of Republicans to the House of Representatives and just enough Senators to make any type of decision-making difficult. The House of Representatives repealed healthcare as promised, then went after abortions, Head Start, and subsidized heating for the elderly while retaining oil subsidies.[28] They went after Gay Rights, Union Laws, Sharia Law (Islamic Law), English as an official language, and of course, my favorite, the light bulb repeal.[29] I was worried there for a moment because I had already invested a lot of money in those new light bulbs and I would have had to discard them all. Remember, our House of Representatives stated that with their election they would produce jobs, jobs, and more jobs. Translation: We will tell you what you need to hear so that you can vote for us and be able to pretend that you are not a racists. Since the 2010 midterm elections, the House has not produced any legislation that would help facilitate job creation and they do not intend to produce any legislation.[30] Like I said before and now will say again, only I will be laughing just a little, job creation is like family values for Republicans. They have no intention of producing jobs and they have no family values other than a mouth full of talk but, it keeps their voters in line. My favorite line from conservatives is that they hate liberals and when ask what is the difference, they usually can't say anything that does not apply to themselves also. That is to be expected since we are all the 99% and in the same economic pot of stew. Dividing the masses always works and has worked for centuries. No sense in breaking traditions.

Governors and state legislatures reduced taxes for the wealthy, increased corporate tax deductions, and started trying to break the unions.[31] It really amazes me that no one has noticed that the only unions that Republicans and Fox News are really going after are the teacher's unions and government employees unions. Let's think about this for a minute. What do those two have in common? Don't everybody answer at once. Those two unions are full of women and minorities.[32] Wow! Who would target women and minorities? Why are teachers always in Republican's sight line anyway? Education is in a bad place but it is not because of teachers only. It sure is not because of President Obama, so don't even start that lie. State legislatures have been cutting school budgets for years and using those monies elsewhere. Since many voters, who have children, don't like the way their children are being educated, they are told teachers are the problem. Get a grip, parents! Your local government is the culprit because teachers give more than anyone should for the low paying job of having to deal with an oversized classroom of your bratty children. (Notice, I said your bratty children because I know my children were angels.) Teachers, then have to make a difference in our children lives, with amenities being taken away every school year. I will repeat myself, the problem with our educational systems is with our governors and our state legislatures.

We are well on out way to the destruction of our middle class, with our permission. We look like we want to fight back with our declaration of the 99%, but are we too late? We elected a bevy of Republican governors who have shown all of their constituents their real agenda which is the destruction of us, the 99%. They have made it as plain as can be that their only concern is that the 1% keeps their wealth and takes what little else there is to take from the 99%. Goodbye to all of our social programs like public education, police and fire departments, Medicare, Medicaid, Social Security, air and water programs, food programs, help for the disabled and poor, school lunches and lunches for the elderly, and infrastructure. Whew! Goodbye to voting. Goodbye to fair redistricting. Hello to privatization of everything so that administrative cost will triple and services will diminish or be eliminated. Hello to Emergency Managers. Hello to the end of the 99%. This is the Republican agenda. This is the true Republican mandate. The proof of their agenda is wherever there is a Republican governor or a Republican legislature. The proof of their mandate is wherever there is a Republican House of Representative or Republican Senator.

Democratic Governor Mark Dayton from Minnesota won the governorship by less than one half of one percent.[33] He tried to combine spending cuts with revenue increases, which would save jobs. The Republican legislature shut the government down.[34] Get it yet, 99%? You allowed yourselves to believe the bull and brought more chaos on yourselves and you did it thinking you would punish the Black President. According to you, you were just the concerned 99%, not the portion of the 99% ruled by prejudices. According to you, these legislators from hell were only suppose to affect minorities and women, not you. Do you get how you have brought about your own downfall with the legislators from hell? Do you understand how this group of politicians is dividing us more and more and more? Do you get that you are not only impacting your future, but your children future?

Just because we are the 99%, we sat and sabotaged our future listening to the false rhetoric. Republican's rhetoric is the President will be one-term. We are told that this is there number one agenda, not jobs or our economic recovery. If that is the desire of the 99%, then so be it. However, if the 99% suffers, gets the shaft, or whatever we have to endure, shut the hell up and grin and bear it. I do not want to hear a peep out of the 99%, not one peep. Fold up your tents and go home 99%. Just because the President is Barack Obama, you elected your own governors from hell, your own legislatures from hell, and your own federal representatives from hell. Just because the President is black you chose to believe those from hell with your eyes wide open. Unfortunately, the only ones who will suffer, from the legislators from hell and our bad decisions, will be the 99%.

WAY TO GO, 99%

Most of these new Republican legislators were elected into office because voters chose to believe that President Obama and Democrats were the responsible parties for our economic meltdown. Voters decided to ignore George W. Bush's Administration and the resulting financial catastrophe and rising unemployment. Voters allowed Republicans to shift the blame to President Obama and the Democrats. Since we had a Black President, it was easy to shift the responsibility. It was easy to con the public since many wanted desperately to believe the worst. Those governors and their legislatures are socking it to the 99% of their state and why not? Why shouldn't they change abortion laws, voting laws, and contract laws?[1] They have mandates, right? I sure felt they had one. After all, what else can anyone assume when the party that was responsible for the economic meltdown is placed back in power, massively, in under two years? When the 99% votes, like they did in the 2010 midterm elections, it's a message that the voters believe in the change that those elected promised. Let me see now, what was that message? Oh yes, I almost forgot for a minute because I was laughing so hard. The message that Republicans told the 99% was "Trust us again and we will produce jobs. We will make the economy better with our agenda, which was responsible for the economic meltdown. We will produce the same jobs that we did not produce for eight years when we were in control. We will also help the wealthy and large corporations because it is obvious that those two entities are the most in need of our help" (giggles). That last part about the wealthy was the real agenda, jobs were thrown in to complete the con job. Therefore, when governors go after bargaining rights, legislators go after abortion rights, and all Republicans say "No" to everything that the President proposes, it is okay because Republicans have their mandate from the 99%. Way to go, 99%.

No one can complain because everyone was told the Republican's mandate well before election day. Republicans let everyone on the planet know that nothing, and I mean nothing, was going to come to the floor unless the tax cuts for the wealthy was extended.[2] Remember that? All Senate Republicans signed a no tax increase ever pledge. Remember that?

Republicans let the 99% know that their only concern was the President being a one-term President. Remember that? In 2010, the Bush tax cuts were so important that Republicans gave President Obama most of the bills they were holding hostage. The Don't Ask, Don't Tell Repeal Act passed. The 9/11 Responder Bill passed. The Small Business Bill passed. The Arms Treaty Bill with Russia passed. So, there was never any doubt about the Republican's agenda. Everyone knew that those tax cuts were their Holy Grail.[3] Remember that? Republican governors pushed laws that continued to degrade the rights of unions, teachers, and public employees. They told everyone that they had a mandate. Remember that? Unfortunately, voters ignored history and all of the rhetoric, so everyone got what they voted for, right? I was not surprised when the Republicans refused to vote to end those corporate subsidies.[4] Especially those subsidies to the oil companies with their profits of billions each quarter[5]. Of course, the farm subsidies could not be eliminated either because Congressional representatives know how much their families, who have those subsidies, would need this form of welfare.[6] Looks like conflict of interest to me. Oops, I had better not call those subsidies welfare because then poor people might apply. I thought that Republicans would have at least pretended that they felt our pain, but that did not happen. Think about it, why would Republicans fake feeling our pain when we told them, with our 2010 vote, that we agreed with everything they were going to do to us? Way to go, 99%.

Republicans voted for spending cuts only and no revenue increases. Revenue increases would have affected their buddies, the 1% and large corporations, aka, the job creators.[7] Spending cuts would only affect public education, police and fire departments, Social Security, Medicaid, Medicare, and any program that helped the less fortunate.[8] Does everyone understand the Republican agenda yet? It consists of tax cuts, loopholes, and subsidies only? Republicans have been 100% honest about this agenda. Here is a great issue that needs to be addressed and for some reason no one makes Republicans answer this question. If the tax cuts are necessary for the job creators and no jobs are created, then why are the tax cuts still in existence? If the tax cuts are necessary for deficit reduction, then why is the deficit still rising? Obviously, none of this makes sense and I am a stickler for things making sense. Where are the complainers? Oh, FOX News, where are you? Oh, Tea Party, where are you? Oh, 99%, where the hell are you? Is the 99% quiet because of buyers remorse? Way to go, 99%

The Ryan budget plan should have made all of the voters of the 2010 midterm elections ecstatic because this plan is the ultimate Republican plan. This is the budget plan that all Republicans are required to endorse. The Ryan plan would mean trillions for the rich and pain for everyone else.[9] Republican Ryan stated that Democrats were demonizing his budget by informing the public that Medicare would be eliminated with his Plan. Since many of the 99% can not and will not believe anything other than what Republicans tell them, then the Ryan plan should be a done deal. Therefore, I will attempt to explain this plan in everyday terms to those who are not quite sure about this bill. Grandma, you just found your death panel. Republicans kept telling you that the Obama Health Care Reform was your death panel. They just got their plans mixed up because they knew that seniors were suppose to be eliminated somewhere. The death panel is actually the Ryan Plan and I am not demonizing anyone because I can read. I graduated from college. Okay, I admit I was being snippy about that reading and college thing. It use to be you could make that statement about high school graduates but not any more, thanks to our conservative legislatures and their constant need to cut school spending. Okay, back to the death panel. Remember, Republicans were initially against any form of health care from a Black President. They hoped to convince the 99% to dismiss his healthcare plan because of the end of life provision which they tried to infer was a death panel. However, it just happened to be the same as the end of life provision in Medicare. They almost succeeded in fooling the the 99% like they did in the 2010 midterm elections. However, the Ryan plan is the real death panel because his plan will eliminate all of Medicare including the end of life provision. It's also a cutting machine. There are tons of cuts to social programs. However, for some reason, Representative Ryan could not include or recommend any revenue ideas. Probably because he signed that "No increase in taxes" pledge." If enacted, the Ryan Budget would accomplish the real goal of conservatives which is tax cuts to the 1% and reduction of government services to many of the 99%. Way to go, 99%.

The 99% is really getting what they ask for every time we have a hostage situation. To restrict what the political system can produce, several self created crises have been enacted just to keep the 99% in chaos. Right after the 2010 midterm elections, Republicans threaten to put people on the street on Christmas Eve by cutting unemployment payments if they did not get the Bush tax cuts for the wealthy extended.[10] The American people were the victims with their threats. In April of 2011, a potential government shutdown was announced.[11] Federal workers were given instructions on how to handle their furlough and senior citizens were sent into a panic about what would happen to their Social Security and Medicare. All of that occurred over the continued resolution to fund the government, that Republicans were holding hostage, to extract spending cuts. Republicans turned a routine debt increase into an imminent and dangerous crisis of taking the country to the brink of default.[12] The debt crisis had been increased several times during the Bush Administration and not a peep out of Republicans until President Obama. The final Republican instigated crisis of 2011 was the payroll tax cut extension.[13] The payroll tax cut was passed in December 2010 and was a part of the President's 2011 Jobs Bill.[14] Knowing that the President works very hard to keep taxes low for the 99%, Republicans decided to object to the payroll tax cut. They insisted that the payroll tax cut needed to be offset by spending cuts. I hope the 99% remembered when Republicans stated that their tax cuts for the 1% did not need to be offset because those cuts made the economy vibrant.[15] It sure seems that the tax cut for the 99% would make the economy even more vibrant. Finally, terrified Republicans pressured the House and they caved. At each point along the way, the stakes have gotten higher and higher. The fate of the unemployed, the fate of everyone that works for the government, the fate of global financial markets, and the fate of the working 99% were all held hostage. Each time these self created crises have been wildly successful in causing chaos. Each time their demands have been met and each time they have the incentive to demand more. Republicans can act this way because the 99% gave them their mandate in the 2010 midterm elections. Where will it end? Doesn't really matter because the 99% got what they ask for with their 2010 vote. Way to go 99%.

You got what you ask for, 99%. I guess everybody is happy. I'm still laughing so we know I am happy. Republicans have shown everyone that there concern is not about improving our economy. Did they enact one jobs bill in 2011? The President's failure is more important than our recovery. What makes all of this so sad is that the 99% keeps buying into the bull. They believe the bull that the President is not a leader especially when the government is in gridlock. A gridlock that many of the 99% voted into office. Somehow, the 99% pretends they can't see the obvious. Maybe, the 99% is ashamed of the way they were conned into the foolish decisions they made in 2010. I know I am ashamed. I never thought the 99% would allow the rest of the world to witness their racism since the 99% swears we are a true democracy. Way to go, 99%.

Just because we are the 99%, we got what we ask for which was more jobs, oops, I mean more governmental gridlock. Nobody can complain because even my grandchildren, who are not and have never been political, can figure that if you put more dissenters in the mix, compromise is not accomplished. Don't try to place all of this gridlock on the President because the 99% and the 99% alone elected this chaos. So, 99%, you got what you ask for. You pretended that your votes were for more bipartisanship knowing that Republicans would not work with this President. You decided to put in those who told you they would not ever compromise and you got what you ask for, no compromise ever, ever, ever. The economy is in the tank because you got exactly what you asked for and voted into office. Here is a great solution and we will really get what we ask for. Vote wisely and only send people to Washington who will work to create jobs and implement shared sacrificing. That will truly be the way to go, 99%.

I Sure Hope You're Satisfied

It's getting wild out there. The misinformation has been in high gear for some time with the President being the number one recipient. Now the Occupy Wall Street crowd is being villainized. FOX News and the right-wing noise machine are trying to castrate and denigrate the 99% out of the fear that the 99% will unify. Any effort to represent the 99%, like the President, always results in massive lies, innuendos, and a ton of misinformation. Isn't that what has happened to the President?

One of the first things that we, as the 99%, must do when we get our majority back, if we get our majority back, is insist that news agencies tell the truth. It needs to be the responsibility of our local news shows and newspapers, like my Miami-Herald, to fact check and explain when people are being misrepresented and their message distorted. No fudging the facts and if errors are made, a retraction is issued in the same time slot that the fact fudging occurred. This is the only way that we can made sound judgments and maybe, just maybe, we can believe what we hear on television or read in our papers. The time of not paying attention is over. Thanks to the black man for making us more aware of these practices because nobody has had as much misinformation as President Obama. I'm sure he has set a Guinness World Record. Therefore, I am going to perform my duty as the know-it-all old black woman and dispel the lies. You can trust me because as a senior citizen, I have nothing to gain.

Republicans like to lie and infer that the President is a Muslin and that is not true. There is no way that the President could be a Muslin without someone seeing him on a prayer cloth or with a Koran. Plus, there is no way that Bill and Hilary Clinton would have missed that tidbit in the Democratic primaries. An issue was made about Republican contender Mitt Romney and his Mormon faith and it was stated that many Evangelical Christians could not vote for him because of his faith. That would also be true of a Muslim, especially after 9/11. We talk religious tolerance but that is not a practice. The backlash from all of the 99% to the President for that lie would have been off the chart and there would have been no way to keep it a secret. I hope we can finally put that issue to rest.

Republicans like to lie and infer that the President is a socialist because of his tax policies. The President's tax policy relies on the same progressive approach that has been the cornerstone of American tax policy since the federal government first collected an income tax in 1863.[1] His policies are not socialist or fascist. The sole intent of these accusations is to keep the 99% divided and confused. Many of the President's policies are a combination of the ideas presented by Democrats and Republicans. Just because Republicans are saying "NO" on issues, that they once sponsored or voted for, does not make those ideas socialistic now that the President is presenting them. This tactic is being employed to put fear in the 99% because when the 99% is fearful they do crazy things like allowing their government to invade another country. Republicans also love to call the President a liberal. They call him the most liberal senator ever.[2] Please, get real! President Obama was not in the Senate long enough to be the most liberal ever. He is not even in the top ten. Democrats are liberal and Republican are conservative, right-wing nutjobs. Oops, sorry, I got a little carried away. The only exceptions to these liberal/ conservative rules are Democrats who run as conservative Democrats but are actually Republicans. They usually run as a Democrat when the slot for Republican is already filled. This never happens with Republicans. They do not have any liberal or Blue Dog, oops, I mean Red Dog Republicans.

Republicans like to lie and infer that President Obama is on the largest spending binge in US history. I'm sure this is just an oversight because that would mean that Republicans forgot 2000-2008 with their spending binge resulting in the huge debt that President Obama inherited. President Bush and Republicans racked up $6.4 trillion with their new policies, tax cuts, and unpaid for wars and programs.[3] The swing from President Clinton's surplus to President Bush's deficits added more debt in eight years than all previous administrations in the history of the nation.[4] President Obama, upon entry into office, inherited $14 trillion worth of debt. President Obama is responsible for 1.4 trillion in debt of which most dealt with the economic crisis Republican policies created.[5] Therefore, if Republicans are accusing the President of a spending binge, what would they call their unbelievable mismanagement of funds? Could it be fraud, maybe? I think this misinformation is the most insulting because it assumes that the 99% is so lazy and stupid that they do not remember President Bush's Administration. It assumes that we are such nothings that we would know the truth and accept the made up version. It assumes that we are admitted racist (giggles).

Republicans like to lie and infer that the reason businesses are not hiring is because of all of President Obama's regulations. The President is revamping hundreds of existing regulations to ease the burden on businesses. The President has said that he is willing to review bureaucratic red tap for cost, benefits, and job creation. However, many complaints are unfounded and driven by lobbyist and industry groups.[6] Republicans deregulated, during the Bush Administration, and caused a financial meltdown along with losing jobs.[7] Yes, there have been more environmental rules but those are for our benefit. The Environmental Protection Agency (EPA) plans to curb greenhouse gas emissions and keep our environment safe. This is fine with me. I don't want to get cancer from contaminated rivers and other waters. I don't want to spend time on the beach and end up glowing because of radioactive materials in the ocean. America is in the top ten countries producing cancer and a great deal is because of altering the environment.[8] Republicans have tried to link our economic downturn with over regulation instead of their under regulation of corporations. Republicans want fewer regulations while allowing businesses to contaminate the environment, our products, our food, and our safer way of life. One recent example of a regulation being ignored resulted in massive destruction of wild animals. Governor Kasich, of Ohio, refused to sign a regulation about people keeping wild animals. Wild animals were let loose and had to be destroyed.[9] When this governor from hell was asked about the regulation, he claimed he did not have the time to implement the regulation. However, the very next day after the massacre, he somehow found time and signed the regulation. I'm sure no one has forgotten the Gulf oil spill. It was a disaster for the Gulf area because of deregulations. Republicans rejected making British Petroleum (BP) pay $10 billion for the cleanup.[10] President Obama gently convinced BP to give him $20 billion.[11] I am still laughing over President Obama's maneuverings. Two weeks before a another coal ash disaster, Republicans passed a bill to block the EPA from regulating coal ash and decided to allow states to make their own standards.[12] On October 31, 2011, there was a coal ash disaster which sent toxic coal ash spewing into Lake Michigan, which is a drinking water supply for Wisconsin, Illinois, and Indiana. I sure hope everyone is still boiling their water. Which proves my point that deregulating just to have no regulations is foolish and dangerous. So let's not ever forget 2000-2008 which is solid proof that deregulation is not the answer.

Republicans like to lie and infer that the President is trying to divide the county through class warfare. The President wants the 99% and the 1% to contribute to our recovery and that is not class warfare. Most of the 99% are not buying this bit of ridiculousness. The 99% knows we bailed out the "Too big to fail" companies. Now, those who were rescued feel that they do not have to contribute along with those who bailed them out of the economic disaster. Translation: The 99% bailed out the 1% and we never even got a thank you note. There are numerous ways that the 1% can contribute and say thank you. About 2.4 million dollars is what the top Hedge Fund manager, John Paulson, made in one hour yet he pays less taxes that the average American. With the elimination of just one of those hedge fund loopholes our government could make over 44 billion in ten years.[13] The 99% would say "You are welcome." One day of the tax cuts for the wealthy will feed the poor for a year.[14] The 99% would say "You are welcome." If the 1% pays Social Security for the entire year, Social Security will have new life.[15] The 99% would say "You are welcome." Getting rid of subsidies, which obviously oil companies do not need anymore, will save billions. The 99% would say "You are welcome." There are so many ways that the 1% can contribute and say "Thank you" and there are so many ways we can say "You are welcome." There is no need to call shared sacrifice a war unless you want to admit that Republicans and the controlling 1% are at war with the 99%.

Republicans like to lie and infer that President Obama is leading the country in the wrong direction.[16] Because the economy is not cooperating, the 99% has bought the lie. As soon as the President took office, this lie started with the Tea Party. In that time frame, President Obama had not been in office long enough for him to lead the country in the wrong direction, but it did not matter. Only the misinformation was important. Forget those nasty little time lines. Now, in 2011, over 50% of the 99% have bought the wrong direction lie and ignored those Republicans, who actively worked against the economy from 2009 to 2011. Once again, the 99% divided itself. Many blame the President for the Troubled Asset Relief Program (TARP) which started in 2008 with President Bush.[17] Many of the 99% blame our deficit on the President's Healthcare Bill which does not go into full effect until 2014. Republicans push the idea that President Obama's policies have lead to $14 trillion in debt which he inherited from

President Bush.[18] Republicans also blamed the President for the stimulus not working. Let's see now. Why didn't the stimulus produce more jobs? Oh, that's right, the states used every dime to balance their budgets.[19] Here is what the 99% seems to have forgotten. We were slowly producing jobs with the President's policies and initiatives and in November 2010, the 99% hijacked itself, believing all of the misinformation. The 99% tied the President's hands behind his back and then sat and complained because the recession, which we were well on our way out of, returned. On March 15, 2010, according to Diane Sawyer of ABC news, in two decades, as unions decreased, working class salaries rose only 20%. However, health care rose 155%, housing 56%, and college 43%. On October 26, 2011, according to Diane Sawyer with ABC news, the wealthiest income has risen 275% in the last two decades. Where has the thinking 99% been hiding? This President has not taken the country in the wrong direction because we had already taken ourselves in the wrong direction. Why has the 99% allowed itself to be so shamelessly manipulated? Why do we believe, at this time in history, after all of the years of wrong directions, it all comes down to one lone black man?

Republicans like to lie and infer that the President is not a leader. In order for this President to be a one-term President, this lie is essential. So, here is a test for everyone. I want every American to take four friends and convince them to follow him or her. Those four friends will not follow him or her even if it means they lose their life. Now, can anyone tell me how they will convince their four friends to follow them? The 99% decided to allow their stupidity and their racism to take them back over the cliff just because Republicans are masters at misinformation. Republicans have convinced many of the 99% that our slow economic recovery is the President's fault even though they have publicly shown everyone that they are the party of "NO" and every form of obstruction. None of this is about leadership. All of this is about the President being a one-term President and the 99% being divided enough to control.

Republicans like to lie and infer that President Obama does not like Jews. Really, where did that one come from? Oh I know, it started when the President had a meeting with Netanyahu of Israel about the 1967 peace agreement and the borders that were recommended and agreed upon. Even I know that the President wants to help Israel and Palestinians reach agreements that will keep them safe.[20] He did not advocate anything different than any other President however Republicans could not miss an opportunity to misinform. It also might convince Jewish voters to switch parties. Well, I guess it might work. After all, Republicans convinced members of the teachers, policemen, and firemen unions to vote for Republicans despite the fact that the party had been demeaning unions for years. A black man is a powerful motivator (giggles). Sorry, sometimes this misinformation is so ridiculous that I have to laugh, but I'm calm now.

Republicans and their right-wing critics like to lie and infer that the President takes a lot of vacation. Nobody on the planet takes more vacation than Congress and they have accomplished absolutely nothing other than to send through a ton of legislation about abortion. Why are Republicans so fixated on women reproductive rights? Anyway, compared to other presidents after 31 months in office, President Obama has used 61 days, Reagan 112 days, and Bush II 180 days.[21] I guess those facts should shut the right-wing noise machine (Never). Why stop making up lies when they work so well? The 99% certainly bought all of the lies in the 2010 midterm elections. Am I mentioning that enough?

Republicans like to lie and infer that the President is a failure in his world policies. Are we drunk on the atmosphere? We almost lost respect around the world because of the Iraq War and somehow Republicans want us to believe the President is not succeeding in other parts of the world? The President took the time to try and mend fences around the world with our allies and our Arab neighbors. Republicans claimed he was sympathizing with fundamentalist who wanted Islamic law around the world.[22] Well, guess what, apparently Arab youth decided that they admired the President so much that they wanted what they thought he had, which was a democracy, acceptance, and the opportunities to live their lives in freedom. This President will never get credit for the Arab Spring, that resulted in several Arab countries disposing their dictators. However, I am giving him full credit. If President Reagan can get credit for the fall of the Berlin Wall, President Obama gets credit for Arab Spring. Good grief, I am just too much (giggles)! Remember the hoopla over the President and the First Lady's fist bump. FOX News inferred that it was a terrorists fist bump.[23] Well, stop the presses because our children are all terrorist because they fist bump all the time.

Republican hopefuls like to lie and infer that the President does not understand the middle class. Presidential hopeful Mitt Romney loves to make this statement along with many other inaccuracies. Mitt Romney loves to infer that the President does not know how to be a leader because he was only a community organizer.[24] I guess Mr. Romney did not understand the need for the President to understand the problems of the 99% by living in their shoes. The President was a Harvard graduate and he had many options after graduation. Luckily, the President did not choose to employ with an equity firm like Bain Capital and dissolve companies while firing thousands and making millions in profit for himself, like Mr. Romney. Another Presidential hopeful Newt Gingrich likes to lie and infer that the President is the food stamp President. His targeted audience of food stamp usage is the African Americans community as he ignores the statistics that prove that most food stamp users are White Americans. Mr. Gingrich also chooses to ignore the fact that the financial meltdown, initiated by President Bush and Republicans, is the real reason for increase in food stamps.[25] Along with these lies, FOX News love to make up outrageous statements against this President and believe me there has been a ton of them. One of my favorites is FOX News claiming President Obama gamed the system by getting a scholarship.[26] Let me translate that one for everybody. President Obama used his brains to get into college as oppose to George Bush who attended Yale and Harvard because of his daddy, aka, alumni child. Remember, President Bush informed the entire nation that he was a "C" student. Like I said before, there was a lot of hoopla about Affirmative Action and no one wanted to address the real admission line skippers, alumni children. FOX News then tried to make an issue about rapper Common and his invitation to the White House. What a hoopla they made trying to infer that Common was a divisive rapper.[27] Seriously, Common is one step behind Will Smith, who is the cleanest rapper ever. FOX News is establishing itself as an elitist. Oops, that's what they called President Obama but the real elitists are those who believe the 1% should not have to share in any of the sacrificing that is necessary to bring America back to her glory.

Republicans like to lie and infer that just because the President is a liberal, liberals are not family orientated. Rush Limbaugh stated that liberals were okay with Casey Anthony killing her child since liberals believe in abortion. According to Limbaugh, only liberals kill their children.[28] Get over it Rush. Just because your mother may have wanted to abort you does not mean that women should not have a choice in the matter. According to right-winger, the Arizona shooter is a liberal.[29] Ignore the fact that he attacked a liberal Democrat. Wouldn't his target have been someone like

John McCain? When the Norway massacre happened, Wall Street Journal, FOX News, and other fear mongers, all immediately called this a jihad event.[30] They were all set to blame Muslims and keep the fear alive. When it turned out that it was a blond hair, blue-eyed, white man from Norway, whom the Norwegian police claimed was a right-wing fundamentalist Christian, he was accused of being an al Qaeda copycat. Where are we in this world? We are allowing our destruction with these alarmist and their intention to keep us in their pockets with our fears.

I like to tell the truth and infer that this President stands alone. He needs me to tell the tale because the President and I think alike. His appearance of not being involved is just allowing those with sense to ignore the nonsense. There is nothing that anyone can do about those who are obligated to hate this President. Some of this reaction is the need to follow Republicans who keep telling everyone that someone else is responsible for the predicament they created. Most of this is racism. If not racism, what else could account for an entire party allowing such disrespect to themselves? What else could account for conservatives staying in lock step with people who insult them with their insistence that the 1% must be protected on everything and the 99% paying for everything? What else could account for the 99% waiting almost three years before they started standing up for their rights with Occupy Wall Street? What else is there? I would be on the floor laughing if it was not so sad. However, I will not be on the floor crying. I refuse to feel any sympathy for this sector of the 99%.

Just because we are the 99%, I thought we needed to clear up some of the misinformation. I can sum this all up in a few sentences. Do not believe Republicans, FOX News, and any other conservative during President Obama's Administration. Do not take polls, don't complain, and please don't sit back and wait to see what happens next. Let your representative know that you expect him or her to represent the 99% or you will recall them or not re-elected them. That simply means their careers are over. This President should not be left battling for the 99% alone. In order for him to be a one term President, the misinformation is necessary so that the hating 99% and the non-thinking 99% can justify their foolishness. In order for this President to be a one term President, he must be some type of alien because he has a strange name, he is black, his upbringing was exotic, he is determined to reach out to moderate Muslims, or even stupider, he was not born in the United States. In order for this President to be a one term President, the 99% must believe the country is going in the wrong direction though it is apparent that we were already in the wrong direction during the Bush Administration. However, we have to blame the black man not the white man because that is the American way of life. What happened in the 2010 midterm elections, with the constant lies and innuendos, is what drove the economy back over the cliff and there is no reason for anyone to try and pretend otherwise. We are where we are, which most feel is in the wrong direction, because of ourselves. We had better learn to decipher the lies or we will be in for a much longer and more difficult time. As long as we refuse to think, we give our democracy to the fear mongers, haters, liars, and 1%. I sure hope everyone is satisfied.

STATE OF THE UNION

Here is the gist of the state of the union. As much as Republicans think that dismantling unions will make America better, it will not and it certainly will not benefit the 99%. For all Republicans who work at industries, your rights will be eliminated bit by bit until you will be working overtime for free. Oops, is that happening in some states now? Your safety will be at the mercy of corporations who contaminate rivers and put pollutants in the sky. Regulations will be eliminated so that workers can be exposed to asbestos and other cancer causing contaminates. For all Republicans in "Right to work" states or are considering letting your state become a "Right to work" state, your wages will be lower and your benefits will be crappier and fewer. Like it or not, every benefit that we have as workers were painstakingly bargained for by unions. They had to fight and many died for the right to have decent working conditions. For this reason, when I hear other workers, the ones who are not unionized, criticizing unions, I am so shocked. It is the equivalent of a bratty child, who has gotten every toy in the store and then complaining because they got every toy in the store. Degrading those who gave you your job benefits is the epitome of spoiled brats.

Unions played a pivotal role in securing legislated labor protections and rights such as safety, health, overtime, and family/medical leave.[1] We have higher wages in this country because of the collective bargaining by unions. We all have better compensation because of the collective bargaining by unions. The 99% is biting the hand that feeds and protects them. People are trying to pretend that corporations decided to make the work environment better out of the goodness of their hearts and that is not the case. Those who want to criticize unions are those who want to allow corporations to treat us as indentured servants and that is not the American way of life. The 99% needs to step back and stop allowing Republicans and FOX News to put negative thoughts in its mind. The Republican agenda is to destroy unions for two reasons. First, corporations would love not to have to deal with unions and their collective bargaining. Second, unions are traditionally democratic. Therefore, Republicans want to attack the democratic base. This union busting has never been for the benefit of the 99%. This union busting is and always has been about making it easier for corporations and the wealthy to make more money.

However, unions voted for the Republican party in the 2010 midterm elections. Tell me unions, how did that work out for you? Did you get your point across that the economy had not recovered and you were mad? Did you learn who your real friends were, yet? Despite the fact that Republicans have never been pro-union, union members, in the 2010 midterm elections, decided to changed sides and turn the traditional strike line into an unemployment line. This told the tale of the 99%. Here is a group of the 99%, unions, who knew how difficult it was to bring about change because unions fought the mighty battle to get the rights of workers. The first time we get a change in the presidency, unions desert the party. So, when I hear about how they are targeted by every Republican governor and their corresponding Republican legislature, I am tickled. Actually I am laughing again because foolish behavior always deserves an immediate response and this was the absolute best immediate response in the world.

Now the fight to protect unions has to start all over again and this time it will be much more difficult because workers assume that their jobs come with all of their rights and privileges. All of the struggles to get those rights have been forgotten by those who are opposing unions at the present time. All of the rights and privileges that we enjoy are no longer associated with the battles by unions for those rights and privileges. Unions did such a good job that this generation of the 99%, who have no knowledge of history, assumes their job's amenities are naturally occurring, which they are not. All of our working rights and privileges are because of unions. However, it appears that many of the 99% are going to try to go it alone. They are going to disrespect unions and hope that their corporations and companies will treat them as equal partners in the working world. They are going to allow their governors to make their states "Right to work" which will result in lower wages and decreasing the odds of getting health insurance and a pension.[2] As a matter of fact, some corporations love us so much, they have insurance on their employees and that insurance is disrespectfully called "Dead Peasants Insurance.[3] Companies wager on employees lives, expecting to make money when they die. It's just another investment scheme and tax loophole for those companies. The company even keeps the policy when the employee is no longer employed by them.

Did I also mention that this life insurance is payable upon death to the company not the family? Now that is a company that really cares (giggles). States want desperately to be in charge, well here's a start. Instead of hassling unions, strike this type of insurance fraud from the books and make the payments payable to the family.

Just because we are the 99%, we cannot allow anyone to condemn unions and downplay their contribution to the working 99%. We must appreciate those benefits that ensure our health and safety. Those who do not choose to join a union can not buy into Republicans and their misinformation. We can never allow anyone to put a negative spin on any organization that is solely for our benefit. However, it is 2011 and Republicans are into total misinformation about unions. Join the club, unions, you are now in the same situation as President Obama. However, no amount of negativity, no amount of lies, no amount of misinformation will change the necessity of unions or the elected President. The President of the United States of America is Barack Obama, a black man. Tada! Unions are here to stay. Tada! Now I can laugh and laugh and laugh and believe me I am doing just that, because that, ladies and gentlemen, is the state of the union.

You can Trust Me

The 99% is very predictable. If a senior citizen, like myself, can predict the actions of the 99%, surely political analyst, from each party, can figure the key to control. Americans allow their impatience to dictate their unbelievably foolish choices and somehow refuse to listen to the actual rhetoric. Is there anything that can be done to us where we get angry enough to recall and send our representatives home? Over and over again, Republicans informed the entire world that the 99% must bear the brunt of all American debt. Every program that may benefit the 99% must be cut leaving the 1% and big businesses with all of their tax breaks and subsidies. After eight years of bad economic decisions in the Bush Administration and a year and a half of Republicans refusing to work to improve the economic disaster in the Obama Administration, Americans decided to trust them again. The divided 99% trusted again and got burned.

Republicans and the Tea Party all knew that the key to their success would be the first Black President. They knew, with the help of Fox News, they would be able to take any situation and demonize the President just because of his race. They also knew they would get over 30% of the 99% to buy into anything presented to them even if what was presented to them would not benefit them. Negativity at the Black President would be the only requirement. It worked, of course, because race and prejudices are the controlling factors in many Americans way of life. Our economy is in trouble and this is the time for those who can help to get into the game, but that is not the Republican agenda. Their focus is not on real solutions which would be shared participation. There focus is on the 1% and there is little concern for anything else. Corporations and big businesses need to start producing jobs because the 99% is the retail spenders. Banks need to start lending because small businesses are the backbone of the county. The 1% needs to start contributing or they can start losing money also. Trust me, revolutions have started on less, look at history. Yes, it took a long time before revolutions started but no one likes to go back to a harder way of living, especially the spoiled 99%. This is why the 99% is gaining popularity. This is also why the 1% is sending in hooligans to disrupt the movement. It will not help but this is the only response that the 1% knows because historically it always works for a little while. At some point, the 99% is going to register and vote Congress out. It will not just be the President, no way, it will be everyone. It will be Arab Spring only in the United States (giggles).

Our major problems stem from our dividing ourselves and eliminating our majority. Our 99% is manipulated into diving itself with the idea that getting rid of big government will make our lives better. Most states are in debt and being bailed out by big government. Has the 99% figured out who will help pay for disasters, healthcare, schools, policemen, infrastructure, and other services that states need help funding. We are told to hate each other and now we have hatred for conservatives and hatreds for liberals. Small towns are told that they are conservative because they are not big cities. They are told that they have family values and those in the big cities do not have any values. There are just as many serial killers from small towns as there are from big cities, maybe more. There is just as much bullying in small towns as in big cities, probably more. There are just as many pedophiles in small towns as there are in big cities, I'm sure there are more. Even a slum, in the big cites, produces people with family values which, by the way, is not a location thing. We do not differ on every issue. If we could stop allowing ourselves from being manipulated, we could solve all of our problems quite easily. However, we can't release our differences and our representatives know this. They work to keep us divided. This is the reason that Republicans keep pushing small government being better that the big Federal Government, just to keep divisions. Somehow, the 99% decided not to connect the facts that Republicans had eight years to make smaller government and instead increased government considerably under President Bush.[1]

Maybe the next time we are in an economic crisis, and believe me there will be others crises, we will act as the true 99%. Voters decided that Republicans were truthfully depicting the Democrats as the reason that unemployment was high and the housing market had crashed.[2] The only reason voters would feel that way is because they were trying to punish the Black President. Facts proved over and over again that Republicans and their policies were the reasons for our high deficit and high unemployment. Their deregulation of big businesses caused our economic meltdown and the reason we had to rescue those big businesses. Their starting two wars, with one of them not being necessary, was their decision. Their not paying for programs and either of the wars is on them. So, why did Americans get suckered again into more Republican lies?

Republicans promised, for the 2010 midterm elections, to do what they were not capable of doing for the eight years they were in control. They promised they would create jobs and fix the deficit that they were responsible for making. Republicans shifted all of the blame for uncontrolled spending and unpaid for policies, implemented by President Bush and his fellow Republicans, onto the new kids on the block, President Obama and the Democrats. The fact that voters pretended to believe the misinformation showed what I have been saying for two books now and that is the ease of conning the 99%.

Most of my generation of African Americans carry around puzzlement at the constant barrage of ridiculous lies and innuendos that have kept us divided along racial lines. African Americans are entitled to their anger because we have always been the recipients of those lies. For the life of me though, I do not understand the masses, who have it all, with their anger at us. What transgression did we commit to keep a large group of racists forever angry? Did we bring ourselves to this continent? Did we enslave ourselves? Why, two hundred years after slavery and Jim Crow, is this hateful crowd still going strong? Why didn't they die out? Could it be that no matter what obstacles you place in our path we learn to adjust? What is making this anger at African Americans so virulent that the 99% can not see the manipulative rhetoric thrown at them? Why did Republicans go into full blown "We will destroy the United States of America in order to make this first Black President fail" mode. What in the world is the driving force? African Americans do not carry all of this hateful anger. We don't like what is done to us and we carry a normal amount of anger but we don't hoard and separate ourselves. We share, we include all. I hope our younger generation is paying attention to racism in its purest form. You rarely get to see what is in history books and we have been presented with the best examples of racism and diving and conquering of the masses. Pay attention youth of this country! This is not where you want to be years from now. You do not want to emulate my generation, who will destroy your future rather than come together for your generation. Like I said before, this is so sad and my Chi energy is getting upset. However, since I know how to self meditate, I will maintain my Chi again.

The impatient 99% wanted change and is it ever getting change. The 99% listened to the misinformation and, unfortunately, the change is not even close to what the 99% thought they would get. Can I laugh just a little here, pretty please? We are well on our way to becoming a country that is ruled by the the controlling 1%. They will be our rulers with our permission. Bravo 99%! You just gave your democracy away because you chose not to decipher the con. Good job 99%! You just elected and will continue to elect your jailers. Applause to the 99%! You have once again allowed racism to change the course of history. Way to go 99%! You just bought the oldest line in the book, "You can trust me."

Just because we are the 99%, we have to do better if we are ever going to be a better nation. Oprah Winfrey said it best. "When you know better, you do better." At three Republican debates, we saw very bad behavior.[3] At the first debate, the question to Ron Paul was if a man was in the ICU and did not have health insurance, what would he do and someone in the audience said "Let him die." At the next debate, Rick Perry was answering questions about the large amount of executions in the state of Texas and the audience applauded the executions. The next debate showed a video of a gay soldier asking about Don't Ask, Don't Tell and some of the audience booed the soldier fighting for this country. Not one candidate, at any of the debates, asked the audience to show respect for those without health insurance, those on death row, or the gay soldier. It just confirmed that the Republican party has been taken over by racists and haters. I know I have given the impression I am against the Republican party and I completely understand that impression. I believe in the two-party system, actually a three party system would be better only if that third party was the Women Party. However, I am against what the Republicans have allowed their party to become. Just to defeat the President and the 99%, Republicans have lost sight of the prize and in the process they have lost their party. I have no idea how they will get their party back. Who knows? Maybe, once the President is no longer black, they can come back, pretend otherwise, and shake some of the racists from their party. (Maybe, maybe not.) Maybe they like the racist and the haters. All I know is when you know better, you do better. Republicans know better. They simply refuse to do better. Then, maybe, the 99% can hear them when they tell them, "You can trust me."

Oops, Wrong Turn

This will be the shortest chapter of all. I know I promised that earlier and I failed but I keep trying. The 99% has decided, with the help of FOX News and the Republican noise machine, that the country is going in the wrong direction. To be specific, President Obama is taking the country in the wrong direction. According to the polls, 73% of 99% believe the country is going the wrong way.[1]

The first thing we have to do is identify when we made this turn for the worst. This wrong turn occurred in November of 2010. That's right, 2010. I know Americans have decided to blame President Obama for this wrong turn. However, the true culprit is that group of the 99% who decided to return those who were the initiators of the crisis. That same group of the 99%, mad because Washington is not getting along, seems to have forgotten that they sent more of the haters to Washington. That same group of the 99%, trying to cover their foolishness, decided they would blame everyone equally. However, I am here and I will not allow it. Not a chance in hell will I let the 99% get away with being lazy, stupid, nothings and pretending that they are not 100% responsible for every bit of chaos and dissension that is Washington in 2011.

The 99% had two simple choices. All they had to do was send people to Washington to work with the President, who they had just elected. All they had to do was send those who refused to work for the country, that would be the "NO" party and any Blue Dog Democrat, home. That is all the 99% had to do and we would probably be out of this recession by now. Instead, the 99% voted or decided not to vote and gave Republicans the economy back, knowing their track record. The 99% is complaining about their own foolish decisions.

Just because we are the 99%, I promised a short chapter and here it is. If we have taken a wrong turn, then I want the 99% to walk into their bathrooms or any room that has a mirror and look into that mirror. In that mirror, the 99% will see the culprit that is responsible for the country going the wrong way. In that mirror, the 99% will see the reflection of the person who could not wait for a slow recovery, changed midstream, and started our rapid decline into another recession. In that mirror, the 99% will see the 99%. The End.

It's a Deal

Trade deals like our China trade deal were not in our benefit.[1] Diplomats made the deal which resulted in a $273 billion trade deficit to China. We should have put a tax increase on China but China negotiates better. We should have made a credible threat of taxing China at 25% instead of the 2% taxation that we have now. Other countries make a fortune off of our trade agreements. How could we have made trade deals that negatively affected our jobs market? How could we have allowed our representatives to create trade deals that incentivised companies to move our manufacturing jobs overseas? I have no idea. What! Me, the know-it all, has no idea? If I had learned Chinese, then I could have been a part of the negotiations, but I was not invited to the party. This is not a problem for me anyway, this is a problem for our Congress. Remember, they are responsible for bills, funding, and trade deals. So do not, and I repeat, do not let those representatives shift the blame as they love to do so often. They made these deals and they can change these deals because jobs will not return until we make better trade deals. Trade deals should benefit us and not some big American, non sharing, corporation or another country.

Let me present my great idea of how to solve all of our trade deals and our unemployment problems. Let me make the deal. Once again, remember that I am not a businesswoman or diplomat, though I would not mind a diplomatic position in one of the Caribbean Islands. I know, I know, there are no state jobs in the islands but I am giving the solution to our problems so something could be arranged for me. Here is my grand solution. Make companies bring 14 million manufacturing jobs back to the states. I'm sure everyone is saying, "Duh!" I am serious. However, corporations will probably ignore me, so let's make them pay attention. Let's find out how much of each corporation's product we consume. How much of their product do we purchase? If we are responsible for 50% of the purchases of their products, then 50% of their jobs should be here in the USA. Whatever percentage of their profit is because of us is directly proportional to the jobs in America. I thought I would present the solution in an equation. Once again, I will be ignored and that is where the good ole 99% comes into the equation. If a company cannot employ us, then we cannot purchase that product. As a matter of fact, we will be serious about "Made in America" and demand our jobs. There are tons of sites that love to give us more information that we can decipher in a lifetime and these are the sites that can inform us of each company's profits from us. CNN, MSNBC, and even FOX News, though I doubt FOX will participate in this endeavor, can inform us of the companies and our contribution to their profits. This is the way we can demand respect. Since the wealthy 1% and wealthy corporations do not feel they should contribute to help the 99%, then the 99% should not contribute to their portfolios either.

Americans buy more crap than any nation on this planet. We have two and three of everything so we are legitimate consumers. So, let's really be the "We" of "Yes We Can" and help ourselves. Now, I know this will be difficult for those who hate the President, but think of it as helping your white neighbor. I know at least one of your neighbors is white because most White Americans do not live with Black or Hispanic neighbors on both sides of them. So, think of your neighbor. If that neighbor forecloses, this will affect your house. If that neighbor loses his job, you might be the next person unemployed. Let's get in the game and all work together. Or in the famous words of Rodney King, "Can't we all just get along?" Yes, I am smiling.

Imagine how shocked corporations and companies will be when their revenue starts decreasing. Imagine how proud we will be when jobs start coming back to America. Here is the really good part. The 99% gets all the credit. President Obama and Democrats will not get credit. Definitely, Republicans will not get credit. I would expect some of the credit but senior citizens rarely get credit for anything. We will have our mojo back. We will be a majority again. Even more importantly, we will show officials that we are holding them accountable for what they are telling us and what they will do for us, the working 99%. However, we must all remember that with this move, we will become targets of misinformation, lies, and innuendos (Oh, my goodness! We will all be black people. Ha-ha, I got you on that one so everyone can stop panicking). My point is that if we demand jobs for our purchase power then we are making a difference and deciding our own future. If we can decide our future, we certainly can decide which idiot, oops I mean individual, we want to represent us in Congress and in our states. We gain control of our destiny. We are the man. Sorry, I got carried away there for a minute.

Just because we are the 99%, employment for the 99% is necessary to drive the economy. Retail spending will increase and the housing bubble will decrease. When we start working again, we cannot stop there. We must make our representatives change our trade deals, bank and oil subsidies, corporations tax loopholes, our tax laws, and anything that affects our country. We do not want to stop corporations and the 1% from making money but there is never a need to hoard because there is more than enough for everyone. We have to be in charge for just a little while because we all know we will lose interest soon. So, we must go for the gusto. We can do it, especially if we follow my plan. It will take a lot of nerve but I have little doubt that we can because we swore "Yes We Can." Full employment would be the best trade deal ever for the 99%.

PAY UP OR ELSE

I was so tired of hearing about the Debt Ceiling that I was on the verge of pulling my hair out and, let's face it, that would really have been a bad idea. I do not have enough time left on earth for my slow growing hair to grow back. So, I thought better of the hair pulling frustration move. However, the debt ceiling discussions were so annoying. Yes, that's what I said, annoying. The 99% sat on their butts and watched as rogue elected officials held us captive. Their threat was basically a government and world-wide shutdown if they could not get their way. Republicans banked on President Obama not wanting the recession to return full force. They banked on President Obama trying to help the 99%. They banked on the 99% sitting, complaining, and blaming. They hedged their bets and won. So, Republicans acted like the brats they were and stood their ground. All cuts would be for any program that helped the middle class and no new revenue from those who basically have all of the money already. No new revenue from the 1% or anyone who we had to help from the economic disaster back in 2009. No shared sacrifice, only cuts and more cuts for the 99%. Can I say the 99% is lazy, stupid, nothing any louder than I have been saying it? Republicans have told the world that they will take this country down before they work with this President just to make him a one-term President.

Republican faithfuls are the main people who complain about the financial disaster and high unemployment that resulted from Republican initiatives from 2000-2008.[1] Democrats and the President are labeled as big spenders while they attempt to clean up the economic meltdown from those Republican's initiatives. Republicans only want their way which has not yielded prosperous results, at least, not for the 99%. They are adamant about returning to their failed policies or they will make the country default and apparently the 99% is all right with their disruptive behavior. I did not hear of one Republican being recalled or informed that they would not get re-elected. I did not hear one person state that it was the 99% fault because they voted that crowd into office in 2010. I did not vote for this crowd because I have too much common sense. Come on, everyone! Can we at least recall some of those hostage takers just to show our dislike of the way we are being treated? Seriously, how difficult is it to recall? We just did it in Miami-Dade, Florida. We said enough is enough and we showed our representative that we were not going to take it anymore.

Apparently, the country does not feel that enough is enough. Apparently, the country does not feel that job creation is important. Apparently, the country is okay with the Republican's plan of slashing programs that benefit the 99% only, especially Medicare, and not touching the 1% programs, like subsidies, tax loopholes, and tax cuts. Wall Street might have caused the crisis but they are not paying for it in any form or fashion. They made the problem with their greed, forced us to clean up the problem, and then laughed at us as they made more money with their paid assassins, the Republicans.

Did I miss the 2010 mid-term election promises and rhetoric from Republicans? Didn't they complain that the President had not produced jobs (which was a bald-face lie)? Then they promised that they would produce jobs (another bald-face lie). Democrats have put forth bills for job creations and Republicans have rejected them. 118 days after the midterm elections and 118 days after the promise of job creation, not one job creation bill cleared the House of Representatives.[2] The President was forced by Congress to perform their job of writing bills. He submitted a jobs bill in September 2011 of which, as of January 2012, Congress has not passed.[3] So, what are we, as the thinking 99%, suppose to make of this behavior? I keep telling everyone what this is all about. This is about making the President fail and if the 99% fails also, so be it, that's life. No complaining 99%, you have known this for some time and, once again, no recalls. Instead, I hear that the 99% is taking polls showing their dissatisfaction of Congress. Why is the 99% wasting their time on polls? As all can see, polls are not observed by Republicans. They do not care. They have their groupies and the Tea Party. Therefore, if the 99% wants to show their true dissatisfaction, then recall or do not re-elect those who will not work for the 99%. Any official who does care about the 99% can not have our vote.

Stop believing the bull that everyone is at fault. As long as the 99% keeps buying into shared responsibility, it will ignore those who are truly not trying to improve our economy. For those who can not identify the culprits, let me spell it out. The only party who has shown their disrespect for the 99% is the Republican party. They made this economic disaster. They refused to work to resolve this economic disaster. They were rewarded by the foolish, uninformed, unmotivated, and sometimes racist 99%. They promised complete destruction of Medicare, Medicaid, and any social program they could get their hands on.[4] They tried to take the country into a depression with our blessing. They then sat back and watched as the 99% took polls and allowed them to remain in office. We are officially the laziest, stupidest, nothings in the world. Recall these bastards. NOW! Make companies bring half of their jobs back to America. NOW! Or, we stop buying and we will all fail together. If the 1% does not want to share in the economic recovery, even though we saved them in the economic disaster, then we all crash together.

Finally, at the last minute, the debt ceiling bill was signed with the 99% getting nothing but cuts and the 1% getting to keep their tax cuts and loopholes. Uh, oh! What happened next? Standard's and Poor's downgraded us.[5] Immediately, Republicans blamed the President. According to Republicans, the first time we are downgraded is with President Obama (the Black President). Republicans and FOX News were ecstatic. Mitt Romney, a presidential hopeful, immediately said the downgrade was because of lack of leadership. The lies and misinformation were in full force and no one took the time to listen to the reason for the downgrade. Standard's and Poor's stated that the downgrade was because of the Republican deal and because there were no tax revenues on the table. Basically, they said the Republican plan was doomed to fail, which is exactly what the President and Democrats were trying to tell the hostage takers.[6] However, no one could get through to the hostage takers because they smelled blood and went in for the kill. Shortly after the deal was made, the stock markets started crashing and the price of gold started declining. Remember, Speaker of the House John Boehner came out immediately and said he got 98% of what he wanted so this is all on Boehner's, the Tea Party, and the rest of Republicans, who were too scared to object to the hijacking of their party. John Boehner and Republicans, this disastrous debt deal is on your shoulders alone.

Along with this Republican debt debacle, a super committee was formed. This committee would consist of six Democrats and six Republicans. Translation: Six people who would not allow a deal without tax revenues and six people who had signed the "No taxes ever" pledge. Well, we all knew where this committee would end up.[7] The super committee, of course, could not get an agreement. Thankfully, President Obama built in a contingency to the super committee process. Triggers were attached to this committee if they could not get an agreement. Apparently, the pentagon would have to take some deep cuts and many social programs would be saved.[8] Hooray, hooray! Pentagon cuts are good cuts. We are out of Iraq and we are coming out of Afghanistan, so we can cut defense. Let's start by getting rid of all of those non-productive generals at the pentagon because they are sucking up too much money. Lets close some of the bases that are no longer functional. We should be able to make some efficient cuts and save billions. Great job, President Obama! What? That's right I said great job, President Obama! Remember, Speaker John Boehner claimed he got everything he wanted with the debt deal and we lost our rating because of his actions. The actual winner was the President because he will be able to cut the most bloated of all agencies. Did the 99% get a quiet victory?

Surprisingly, I heard that President Obama started losing support as the debt ceiling debate went on and on. I felt like I wanted to throw a dish against the wall because of the stupidity of the 99%. Lazy, stupid, nothings should at least be able to figure this one out. I had the dish in my hand and then remembered who would be expected to clean that mess us and I decided to act my age and just fume, once again. This is not good for me at my age, constant fuming might lead to a heart attack or something, so I write instead. Anyway, the core supporters of the President are mad because the President always appears to be giving away the store. Somehow, progressives seem to have forgotten the 2010 midterm elections, when the President took a shellacking because progressives decided not to show up. How's that working for us all now? The fact that the President is the only adult in the room seems to be something that progressives keep overlooking. The fact that the President is constantly met with a wall of "NO" on everything seems to be another thing that progressives keep overlooking. The fact that this crowd of naysayers are willing to destroy the country and never back down on anything seems to be the biggest thing that everyone seems to keep overlooking. Well, by all means, keep getting angry and threatening to put the nuts back in office. When I hear Americans say that nothing is improving and they will not support the President this time, I say "Go for it." There is never a time when being an idiot is not rewarded. So, by all means, go for it, do just that. Keep pretending that what Republicans have already shown you of their mandate will not happen to you, the 99%. Like I said, I am getting a good laugh and I see I will be laughing all the way through my old age. There is no better example of how progressives will benefit than how unions are benefiting under Republican governors. Excuse me just a moment. I have to get off the floor again because I fell over the chair laughing so hard.

Before the debt ceiling fiasco, we had a few other hostage situations. How many times have Republicans threaten to stop unemployment payments, just to emphasize that they could stop payments? Remember right after the 2010 midterm elections, Republicans reemphasized their threat that nothing would pass until their tax cuts were approved. Then there was opposing the budget, threatening Medicare and Social Security payments, if they did not get their way. What would the 99% have had the President to do? How many would have appreciated having no money when their unemployment was stopped? How many bills like Don't Ask, Don't Tell, Stark Treaty, 9/11 Compensation Bill, and Small Business Bill would not have passed if the tax cuts had not been approved? How many senior citizens would not have been able to have food because their checks were being held captive? It is so easy for the 99% to think the President had choices but he did not and everyone knows that.

Republicans were placed in office because of jobs but it has been one problem after another and the voters are not blaming them for anything. Where are the Republican's jobs? Republicans are holding the House hostage. They don't do anything, they don't pay for anything instead they defund. They held the FAA hostage.[9] They changed the Clean Air Bill and altered the Food Inspection requirements.[10] They are ignoring the Infrastructure Bill and are altering environmental benefits that we had already established.[11] They are punishing the 99% just to make the President fail. So, why is the 99% complaining about the President when we are all being held hostage by Republicans? What did I tell everyone? You get the mess you vote into office. You vote chaos into office, you get chaos.

I know that President Obama has to bend and bend but at least understand that without our support, there is no other alternative. He does not cave, as all love to say, because he just loves to cave but you can not beat a dead horse. I love those old sayings and my generation has a ton of old sayings. I don't know what this young generation will have as their old sayings, though "Sucks to be you" sounds like it is something the 99% will be saying real soon. Anyway, I support the President's idea that he cannot sweat the small things and without any support, he has to make deals. However, he always seems to come out on top for the 99%. Imagine if he had our full support, then we could say goodbye to any type of hostage situations.

Just because we are the 99% and so easily duped, this is my suggestion. Do not participate in any polls, recall, or do not re-elect. There is no other way to show your love other than to say "Get Lost." We all have an advantage that we are not aware of and that is that politicians want the great job of spending hours doing nothing. Think of how great it is for our politicians who take weeks and weeks to pass a bill that could be passed in a couple of hours. Their procrastination means more time for golf, tennis, or even a workout at their exclusive, paid for by the 99%, gym. Think of all of the trips they would miss if they could not do months and months of research on a trivial bill. Think of how many would not become millionaires if they were not in office. Congress is an insider trader heaven.[12] To think that Martha Stewart had to go to jail for insider trading when she could have just run for Congress and stayed a free woman. Think of all the vacation time they have while in office. Think of their children not being able to get into the college of their choice because their daddy is no longer a US congressman. Think about how the 99% can impact the lives of their elected officials just to make their point. Believe me, opinions can change with the correct motivating tools. If the 99% can be held hostage and made to pay up or else, the 99% can change their minds about their representatives. After all, we vote politicians into their illustrious positions. They work for us. We do not work for them. So no more of this hostage crap. Pay up and help this economy or else go home.

IT'S A PRIVATE MATTER

Why do our representatives want to privatize everything? Education, prisons, and Social Security, just to mention a few, are always on the chopping block. Recently, the Post Office went on the block. We constantly hear that education costs the states every dime collected and teachers and their unions are the only reason for the problem. Administrative costs never seem to enter the picture. Why would states assume that prisons are better run by a private company? Are we to assume, just like education, that administrative costs will not enter into the picture? Social Security administrative cost is .09%. There is not a private retirement fund anywhere that will have administrative cost that low. Will the 99% ever understand these privatization cons that keep getting thrown at them? Will the 99% ever learn?

I do have not a PhD, which is required for many of our educational thinkers. I am only a college graduate, class of 67, Fisk University. However, it appears that educational problems are not that difficult. There is nothing that cannot be solved quickly. Every state has "A" schools so all states have the blueprints to quality education. However, everyone pretends that they do not know how to solve the current problem with education because those in power do not want everyone to get quality education for free. See, that is the dilemma. Private schools cannot make a ton of money if people can get free quality education at a public school. You know, that kind of education that baby boomers received for free, back in the day. That same free education which produced educated, constantly complaining, and demanding adults who made a difference to our nation. However, private schools want more of that education money so free education must become a problem. In my state of Florida, testing is mandatory for all Florida students except those who are in private schools.[1] Regardless of their educational abilities, those private school students can graduate without any type of testing. What a sham. I would like to blame Governor Rick Scott because he is my favorite governor from hell, but this was happening before he came to office. Now, if he tried to help his wealthy friends by transferring money to charter schools, then that would be another issue. Oh, my goodness! That is exactly what my governor has done, so I get to blame him after all. He just informed teachers that many will be laid off and then he diverted school funding.[2] I love the duplicity.

Since education is a billion dollar business, our politicians want their friends to benefit and those friends are not the 99%. They are the 1%. Our state legislatures have been taking education monies and using those monies elsewhere and then pretending that teachers are the problem. States have decimated school budgets by paying their staff and themselves ridiculous salaries, giving away subsidies to big businesses, and then shifting the burden on the teachers.[3] Every little municipality wants their own elected officials but that only serves to dilute the funds from the states and the end result is our education system being the victim. Our politicians are using our state budget for stadiums, roadways to nowhere, special contributors homes, and increase in monies to any of their pet projects.[4]

Teachers are the only people who are blamed for our educational system being in a chaotic state. The people who have our children all day long and have to tolerate all types of behavioral problems are the only people to blame. The profession of teaching is demonized to eliminate tenure and justify privatization. Teaching is the profession that has saved the United States of America. Our greatness is due to our teachers. Unfortunately, teachers have also taught a few ingrates because now that those ingrates have money, they feel the need to denigrate teachers. I'm talking about you, Hannity of FOX News, you, Rush Limbaugh, of course you, Bill O'Reilly, and all the others who feel the need to disrespect teachers. Shame on you all and just to understand my true feelings, a pox on your soul. (I'm reading other classics now, thus the pox statement. I feel better already.) We allow our politicians to shift their responsibility of managing educational money properly and blaming teachers, who are poorly paid for the massive responsibility of raising our children. The answer to our educational problems is not privatization. When we divert our educational funds, the only winners are the private companies that will get those contracts. Remember, not everyone is going to get those educational monies. The 1% will get the biggest piece of the pie.

Next in line is the privatization of prisons. Prisons are the counterweight to education. If we educated properly, we would have a smaller prison population. Prisons are big money making businesses and that is why so many are privatized or being privatized. Americans gain absolutely nothing from privatization other than added expenditures without our oversight. Privatization will cost us big time and of course the only place that money can be diverted will be education.[5] See how that works? It will be working in every state soon.

Privately owned prisons need to make sure that their cells are full because that is their profit. The number of people in privately owned prisons have risen 120%.[6] Last year the nation's two largest privately owned prisons made nearly $3 billion. If there is that type of profit margin from prisons, why wouldn't states make the $3 billion in profit and use it for their states? Why turn over that type of profit to someone else? Private prisons pay politicians to enact bills to put people in prison and keep them there longer. Arizona passed the strictest immigration law so that their private prisons could make a profit. Immigrant incarceration keeps the beds filled in Arizona's private prisons.[7] Lawmakers raked in 14.6 million in donations from private prison lobbyists.[8] We spend 3 times as much imprisoning people than educating people.[9] Why are we cutting schools and firing teachers just so that private prisons can make a profit?

This is one of the reasons Republicans are so eager to privatize Social Security. They see this program as a money pit for their greedy friends. All of this talk about this program being bankrupt is a big old fat lie. Social Security has been one of the governments most effective programs.[10] The costs of Social Security is funded on its own dedicated revenue. There is no deficit financing. The administrative cost is .09%. It returns 99 cents on every dollar collected. The administrative costs of a private company will never be as low as the government. Higher administrative costs means less for the recipients. If Social Security is running our of money, then we need to look at Congress. We need to find out if Congress has been raiding the fund. You know the famous saying. "Rob Peter to pay Paul." How much of our money was diverted for a war or some unpaid program? We will never know.

The Post Office, of "Neither snow, nor rain, nor heat, nor gloom of night," is in jeopardy. The Post Office does not use any federal money. The Post Office is mandated to go where others refuse to go and usually gets bitten by a dog to prove it. The Post Office works. The Post Office makes billions in profit however almost all of their losses over the last four years can be traced back to a restriction forced on them by the 2006 Republican-led Congress.[11] So, why did the 2006 Congress pass a bill to take money from an organization that does not get any federal money?

Obviously, because they can. The Post Office was forced to pay their pension for 75 years in 10 years. This meant that the Post Office had to set aside billions to pay benefits for employees who had not been hired yet. What other company, not getting tax money, is forced by Congress to do that? Congress does not even do that for programs that are getting tax money. So, are they using Post Office money for other agencies? Guess who gets to hold the money? That's right, Congress gets to hold the money. Will they use the Post Office monies properly or will they use it like they used Social Security monies? In 75 years, will the Post Office still have any of their pension monies or will those idle funds be used for shortfalls in government spending? Well the "Blame everybody else Congress" will never tell. This antic was just the Republican way of sending the profits from mail to the two companies who contributed the most to their campaigns. Republicans have been getting big bucks from FED-EX and UPS.[12] However, those two do not go to small farms and out of the way places. Guess what! They give those letters to, you guessed it, the Post Office, who will be replaced with privatization. I guess rural Americans will have to move to the big bad cities just to get their mail.

Privatization is a biggy with Republicans. Privatization is Republican speak for ridding the country of big government. When everything is occurring at the state level, people will be discriminated against. I know, I know, most are okay with that because they feel that Black Americans will be the only recipients of the discrimination. Well, think again. This time around we are all going to be discriminated against. Remember, the government will be controlled by the 1% and, unfortunately, they do not care about any of us. Granted the discrimination will be tiered, with Black Americans getting the worst, as usual, but White Americans will also get the shaft. Without a centralized form of government, we will all be in for the slippery ride into more chaos. We will not have anyway to decipher the truth because our news agencies will be tainted. We will hear all kinds of untruths depending on who owns the television station, radio station, or newspaper. Yes, the internet will be compromised also. Actually, the internet and some of our news agencies are already full of crap.

There is no proof that privatization will save the government a dime. Administrative cost will always factor into these contracts and we will pay more for our new privatized Federal Government.[13] Without a centralized form of government, what happens when disasters hit? Will we privatize the Federal Emergency Management Agency (FEMA)? What happens when Florida gets hit by a hurricane in June, July, and August? Florida can't pay for the first hit but three hits would be too much. What happens when Kansas gets hit by twenty tornadoes all over the state? What happens when California gets hit by earthquakes, floods, fires, and mud slides? (I was thinking of moving to California and decided that Florida is actually luckier with hurricanes. At least, I have time to hide.) My point is that states who do not have a lot of natural disasters will not want to use their precious funds bankrolling adjoining states with their constant natural disasters. If 48 out of 50 states are in debt now, without having to pay for their natural disasters, how will states fare cleaning up after hurricanes, floods, tornadoes, mudslides, and any other thing that Mother Earth can throw at us? Sort of seems like Mother Earth is telling us to "Clean up your act or I will punish you." However, it could just be my imagination.

Republicans have already made a stink over paying for storms and other disasters.[14] They want offsets. If we are privatized, who pays for these freak disasters? I remember when New Jersey's Governor Christie was talking real big and bad about how the Federal Government needed to be more frugal and learn how to manage its money. He was touted as a brash tell-it-like-it-is governor. Then Hurricane Irene hit and suddenly Governor Christie was not interested in the Feds being frugal. As a matter of fact, he even jumped on his fellow Republicans and basically told them to shut the hell up until his state was compensated.[15] After all, the situation had changed. Now, his state needed help. As long as Florida was being hit by hurricanes or California was being hit by mudslides or earthquakes, and those states needed help, the government was being wasteful. It seems to be different when lawmaker's states are hit by disasters, which is essentially what Governor Christie was saying. Getting help from big old bad Federal Government would suddenly be okay because there was no way he was going to have his voting constituents suffer.

The answer to our problems is not making government smaller. Improving government is much more economical. Privatizing government is certainly not the answer. Private companies have much larger overhead than the national government because they feel they have to pay their CEO's ridiculous salaries.[16] It had been reported that American CEO's make 475 times as much as their employees as opposed to Japanese CEO's who only make 11 times as much as their employees.[17] However, allowing our government to misuse our trust and our tax dollars is also not acceptable. We can rid our government of waste by starting with bringing home those elected officials who waste federal funds appealing laws that are already on the books, like healthcare, clean air, and all the other bills that are beneficial for the 99%.

Just because we are the 99%, a centralized government is our insurance of fairness. It ensures that all states have the same educational opportunities and the same standards. I would hate to move to a state with my family and their educational standards were severely different. My child might be in grade six in my old state and grade four in my new state. Standards are important. A centralized government ensures that all states have social programs. It ensures that every aspect of our lives is available in any state. The Federal Government, economically, takes care of the country ensuring that all Americans get equality in all matters. It basically ensures that someone always has the back of the 99%. Yes, we need to improve on the government but you don't throw the baby out with the bathwater. Hey, I warned you I had a lot of those old sayings. We all can see where we need to improve. So, let's improve instead of replace and privatize. This is a public matter not a private affair. Let's all get back in the game and make the Federal Government the best.

Foreign Affairs

Finally, finally, after thirty years, Arab countries decided that enough was enough. Those countries finally decided they wanted democracy or some facsimile. They wanted jobs, homes, and lives that would not be tempered by fear. Finally, we convinced the world that our example of a democratic government was the only way. Over and over again we told the world of how superior we were because we elected our own government. Over and over again we told the world that we had the right to be anything we wanted to be because we had the right to a free education. Over and over again we told everyone we were the best of the best because of our freedoms. So, why in the world are we shocked that those Arab countries decided to believe us?

No man is an island and no country exist on this planet alone. When other countries try to become as they think we are, we need to help them. How we help them is determined by them, not us. People want to be involved in their own freedom and we have to respect that request. We can not monitor the entire world even though, technically, we actually do monitor most of it. We can not interfere into every skirmish that occurs but we certainly can offer assistance, if requested. We can work with the North Atlantic Treaty Organization (NATO) and the United Nations (UN). We can be a part of the community of nations that want the chaos in the world eliminated or at least dialed down a degree. The world's enemies have been identified and we are all responsible for working to keep those enemies from perpetrating another 9/11 event anywhere in the world.

The first time that any of us realized there might be some type of upheaval was in Tunisia.[1] A young man had his scale confiscated for the umpteenth time by a public official. He was tired of the constant struggle to earn a living and decided to commit suicide. This started the protest in Tunisia that resulted in the ousting of their president of 23 years. We all watched in amazement. Here was the first example of people deciding that they wanted dignity and democracy, and enough was enough. The United States did not have to do anything because this was a people uprising.

Next was Egypt.[2] How spectacular was that to see? The people of Egypt decided that enough was enough also and they wanted change. They wanted a life that was livable and not a struggle. They wanted all the bells and whistles that go along with a democracy. They handled the situation peacefully and luckily their dictator did not try to kill them all as others have tried. Once again, this was easy for America because we did not have to interfere. Egyptians could have the joy of fighting for their way of life. They could have the pride of standing together as the majority and obtaining their freedom. That's what we all want to see, a peaceful demonstration for freedom. However, every one on the planet knew that Egypt was a fluke. They were going to be the golden example not the norm. After the ousting of the president, the military took over and that never bodes well. The people of Egypt continue to fight for their freedom and they are determined, so there is still hope.

Following those two Arab nations were Yemen and Morocco. As of 2012, both are still fighting for their freedom. Yemen has ousted their leader of 23 years and Morocco is just beginning the fight.[3] Hopefully, once people taste freedom, they will not go back.

Libya was next in line for people wanting their freedom. We all knew that Libya was not going to react like Egypt. Kaddafi would never go down without a bloody fight and he would kill as many people of his country as he could and, guess what, Kaddafi lived up to his craziness. The people of Libya requested help from the United States. Why not? Aren't we the only ones with a commanding military? Haven't we been telling everyone that they deserve freedom? Haven't we been telling everyone that democracy is the right of all people? We could not sit and do nothing and that is why the President and the other nations of NATO reacted.[4] Things would not go well for those who wanted their freedom in Libya. Since Kaddafi had plenty of weapons, they were at his mercy, of which he had none. So, we helped and eventually Kaddafi was ousted. Some of the 99%, and that would be FOX and friends, felt that since we had no interest in Libya we should not have intervened. So, if I am to understand this logic, trying to achieve what we have suggested is the best government is not enough justification for our assistance. Did I get that right? Is that the consensus of Republicans, FOX News, and many "I hate the President" conservatives? If we can't use you, we can't help you. Well, that certainly is not a shock to me and it should not be a shock to anyone who is deep into this book. This is the mentality of those who want our rights diminished all in the name of the 1%. I wonder if that crowd understands that they are not the 1%. Well, we all must learn and I hope I am here to see everyone's eyes opened.

Lastly Syria started protesting and, like Kaddafi, their leader is not going to step down without a bloody fight. Hooray to Tunisia, Egypt, and Yemen. Morocco is still a work in progress and Kaddafi of Libya is deceased. Hooray! Our Congress acted ugly through all of the uprisings, like who did not know that. The only Arab nation that we needed to assist was Libya. Libya was deemed an illegal war because Congress did not okay it. Here is the question that I have to ask? Why didn't Congress okay the war?[4] They were okay with the illegal war in Iraq. That war was a quagmire and we lost a lot of soldiers because of the falsity of that war. Then along comes pleas from people who only want democracy and many in Congress decided that we should not help in any way. We only help those who we can occupy and waste a ton of money on as oppose to those who require not one ground troop, just air power. You have to love the thought that we elected this batch of ungrateful bastards. I'm sorry, I did not mean to curse, so delete ungrateful.

As I said before, my thoughts about the Arab Spring are that President Barack Obama gets the credit. That's right, I am giving him credit for Arab Spring because if all will remember, FOX News and many conservatives complained about his insistence on reaching out to Muslims nations. However, he did reach out and let the young people in those nations know that the United States was with them. Those young people saw this attractive, attentive, understanding, and engaging President and it gave them hope and finally the incentive to act in the best interest for their future. Bravo! Like I said before, if we can give credit to President Reagan for the Berlin Wall, which by the way, I do not, then we can give credit to President Obama for the Arab Spring, which by the way, I do.

Osama bin Laden is dead, Hooray, double hooray! President Obama found and killed Osama. Hooray! I know everyone is relieved and I know that all Americans are happy that we finally caught the bastard. Okay, okay, I seem to have referred to Osama and some members of our Congress as bastards and I do not want that term to have equal value. Osama was a godless bastard and Congress are just non-caring bastards. See the difference? Anyway, Osama is dead and somehow FOX News decided to give President Bush the credit.[5] Seriously! When President Obama came into office he inherited banks failing, corporations failing, and one of the biggest economic disaster we have experienced in a long time. FOX News decided that President Bush was not responsible, President Obama was responsible. When we entered into a deep recession from the Bush policies, FOX News decided that President Bush was not responsible, President Obama was responsible. According to FOX News, everything that President Obama inherited from President Bush in 2009 was his and his alone until Osama is killed in 2011. Somehow the Osama killing is President Bush's victory. Like I said before, if you buy that, then come on down and check out this choice piece of land that I have for you in the Everglades. Ignore the gators, and watch out for our newest residents, Boas.

Here is the truth of the matter. Six months after 9/11, President Bush said, from his very own mouth and I heard it, that he was not concerned about Osama bin Laden.[6] President Bush made several statements about how unimportant Osama was and he did not care. He even closed the unit that was hunting Osama in 2006. So, please tell me how FOX News has the audacity to try and give President Bush credit for this kill? How many times can I emphasize the desire by those who hate President Obama to give him credit for anything. They have declared war on the first Black President and this is a historical lesson for the youth of this country. Our youth get to see how the establishment uses their racism to try and change the realities of the 99% by using our public airways to distort and manipulate. To the youth of this country, this is your opportunity to see the way that dictatorships start and survive in so many countries around the world. Don't fall victim to this type of mind control. Don't take these talking heads seriously. Think at all times, reason at all times, and if it does not make sense, do not believe it. Never, ever assume that the news you hear or read is from a free press just because they are in America. A lot of our free press is owned and operated by very wealthy individuals and though I am not trying to insinuate that all are corrupt, because they are owned by the wealthy, but there are a few, and FOX News is the major one.

Next terrorist killed was Anwar Al-Awlaki and then there have been more. This is my observation. President Obama is serious about making Americans safe by eliminating as many terrorists as possible. According to Republicans, they were the only people who could keep Americans safe. Now, I knew that was not true because 9/11 happened on their watch. How they keep convincing Americans that they are the only ones who are security conscious will always be one of the great mysteries of the world.

That was a joke, of course, and I am laughing out loud. There is no reason for Republicans and FOX News to be jealous of President Obama because their talks about security were just another set of their talking points. You know, like family values, pro-life only in terms of the unborn not those on death row, shared sacrificing only in terms of the 99% sharing all of the sacrificing, and job creation, of course. It is not hard to understand Republicans and FOX News as long as you skew logic, which I refuse to do ever.

According to some taking heads, Israel is not pleased with President Obama. They infer that the President is not a friend of Israel because he suggests Israel work with Palestine for a two-state peace agreement. The President is not trying to give the Palestinians a pass, just some form of agreement where both parties can move forward. There is a peace treaty and if one side has not live within that treaty, then that side should be called out. If the treaty made boundary lines, then those lines should be adhered to.[7] One side cannot flaunt the treaty. If everyone signed the treaty, then that is the document that must be followed or rewrite the treaty, but one side cannot just ignore the signed treaty. The world has lived with this situation for years and we help Israel because they are a true democracy. However, if these Arab nations are truly trying to change their countries, we should all be on board because this makes Israel a safer place.

Just because we are the 99%, our majority makes us an integral part of the changing world, which is a good thing. When I was a young person, I was just a citizen of the United States. Now, my children and their children are citizens of the world because of the Internet and it's universal connections. My generation wrote letters and had pen pals. My children and their children email, tweet, and socialized all over the world. No man is an island and that was never truer than at this time in our lives. There are no more foreign affairs because we are all connected. We must help any nation that needs our help. However, we, as the 99%, need to also help ourselves so that we will not end up as a foreign affair in our own country.

GIVE IT A REST

Our nation is in the fight of its life. Instead of our politicians working to improve our economic situation, they are trying to impress their constituents with irrelevant chatter. Twitter is not for politicians. Give it a rest, please! Twitter is for young people in high school trying to talk while they are in class. Facebook is not for politicians. Facebook is for young people getting to know each other. These social medias are young people's domain, not for stodgy old politicians trying to appear hip. The proof of my assertion is how politicians are making total fools of themselves talking like ditwads and getting caught with embarrassing pictures. When you tweet, you have to use abbreviated words and while that is cute with young people, it is just embarrassing for older people. I do not tweet. The reason I do not tweet is partially because I do not want to sound foolish and also because of a statement I read by Carrie Underwood, the American Idol winner. Don't panic, it will all make sense in a minute. When she was asked about tweeting, she said tweeting was like organized stalking.[1] I could not agree more so our politicians should just email and try to act like an adult instead of a high school student. As all can see, sending inappropriate pictures on these social medias can not be performed by politicians because of their ineptness. This is why most get caught saying and doing stupid things. This is also the reason we should make recalling as easy as dialing a phone. We leave these degenerates in office and then wonder why we get absolutely nothing from our government. If we want this process to be a silly season, then by all means continue to leave these unproductive and petty politicians in office and we will all continue to have the government no one wants.

Next in line for giving it a rest is immigration. Hey, I know you are trying to connect social media and immigration but the title of this chapter is not the foolishness of our politicians, it's give it a rest. All Americans are immigrants except Native Americans and African Americans. Give it a rest, please! Native American did not ask other Americans to come to their country and African Americans did not ask to come here, we were forcible brought here. My point is that even though White Americans were not in our boats, when we were brought here, we are all in the same boat now. Let's stop this crap about sending people home because like I said in my last book, Native Americans can tell us all to go home. Let's find a way to incorporate all of our illegal immigrants into the system that they are already a part of. Yes, they did not enter legally. Yes, they took a short cut but we allowed it and we all know it. We allowed it when we let those illegal immigrants pick our crops. We allowed it when we let those illegal immigrants be our cheap nannies. We allowed it when we hired those illegal immigrants as dishwashers, maids, and gardeners. We allowed it and we have no right to now act as though we did not allow it. We teach our children to take responsibility when they mess up. Now, we must practice what we preach. We must enact measures so that millions of illegal immigrants can be a part of our democracy. We must give those immigrants the tools to be legalized, now. Yes, we should secure our borders so that we stem the flow, but we must help those who are already here at this time in our history. This foolish talk of sending people back is not christian and nobody claims to be more christian than those very same people who want to send immigrants back to their country. So, please, give it a rest! Find a way to solve this problem. The first step should be the Dream Act for those young people who were brought to this country through no fault of their own.[2] From there, we can go anywhere as long as we make those millions our new citizens.

Next are the wealthy 1%. Give it a rest! We know you are rich. There is no need to flaunt your wealth in our face. We get it. The really crazy part about all of this is that most of the 99% do not envy your wealth like Republican presidential hopeful Mitt Romney seems to think.[3] Yes, everyone would like to be financially secure but that is really all anyone wants. Wealth appears to drag people down. The wealthy are required to dress better so they must spend a lot on clothes that are never worth the price other than to brag to fellow wealthy people. They are required to drive more expensive cars just so they can have the joy of driving next to a Ford Fiesta on a crowded highway (giggles). They are required to send their children to private schools so that the 99% will not know how dumb their children really are. They are required to have more than one house. They are expected to get a good job even if their daddy has to give them the job. So, as all can see, there are a lot hangups for the 1%. However, it appears that the 1% cares more than we do. Why the need to buy politicians? I understand their need to buy a few policemen when their child gets caught with drugs but why waste the money on politicians? After all, politicians are elected by the 99% and surely the 99% would not allow politicians to ignore them to the detriment of the wealthy 1%. Ha-ha, that was one of my best jokes ever. I know the 1% never figured they would be so obviously in control. Who knew that Republicans would be so blatant? Who knew they would con the 99% so easily? Well, actually, I knew because the President is black. However, now that the 1% has control, has it been good for them? I would say "Yes it has." They have a lot more money and they have not had to share a dime. They can get around all of those pesky US regulations by sending jobs elsewhere and still get a tax cut. They are greedy and greed always seems to lead to more greed. They have more money than any other time in history but there is one real problem and that is they will not go to heaven. That's what the bible says. It says "It is easier for a camel to go through the eye of a needle than for a rich man to enter into the kingdom of heaven."[4] Of course, if the wealthy shared, maybe there might be a slight chance. However, enjoy your few years of being the 1% and then enjoy your eternity in Hell. Ha-ha, the 99% gets the last laugh.

Give it a rest, Wall Street! Many on Wall Street hate the President which is odd since they have not suffered during this economic crisis. They were totally responsible for the economic meltdown and no one went to jail thanks to the rules set in place by the Bush Administration.[5] No one paid the price for their manipulations of statistics to put lots of money in their pockets and the pockets of their investors. They won big time and now they have the audacity to expect their bad behavior to be rewarded with more deregulations. Some of the 1% also do not like the President and they have also profited. The desire to control everything through wealth is a bad move. The 99% will not take to poverty very well. Allowing people to have enough money to buy the products produced by the 1% is necessary for the 1% as well as the consumers, which would be the 99%. Shared responsibility is an absolute necessity for this country and at some point the 1% needs to contribute. The CEO of Starbucks said he is going to continue to add jobs. He wants the 1% to stop contributing to politicians until they act like true representatives of all of the people.[6] Even Warren Buffet said the 1% needed to contribute more. So, I say this to the 1% and big corporations, "You can't take it with you" and you can't get into heaven anyway (giggles). This is the time to act like you care and contribute. Believe me, Republicans will make sure that you do not contribute too much. Give it a rest, 1% and Wall Street! You have more than enough to share in our recovery.

Give it a rest, Republicans! If we do not have individual mandates for our Healthcare Reform, who will pay for those who do not have insurance? This is the one question that no one answers. Who covers the expenses of hospitals, doctors, and nurses? Who pays? Until Republicans can answer that question, then leave the Obama Healthcare Reform alone. Republicans have not written any healthcare initiative to replace Obama's Bill. They simply want to repeal the bill so that they can, once again, get their way over this black man. However, they are not telling anyone who will foot the medical bills of those who do not have insurance. I'm listening Republicans. I have an idea and that is to be expected. Leave the bill alone and work to make it the best it can be. Ha-ha, we all know that will never happen but I thought I would give it a try.

Just because we are the 99%, we are in charge of getting our democracy back. We can continue with our foolishness or we can give it a rest and make this country the great nation that we have come to expect. We must unify our 99%. The choice is all ours but the 99% will have to stop complaining about things that it can change itself. The 99% must take responsibility for the 2010 midterm elections and admit that we interrupted our slow recovery. We must admit that we voted the dissension and chaos into office. We must admit that we allowed misinformation to influence our thinking because of our subconscious racism. We must look at the entire picture and understand that our progress was stalled by no one other that the 99%. Then and only then can the 99% give it a rest.

THE PLEDGE

"I pledge allegiance to the flag," is a pledge to our country. "I pledge my troth," is a pledge in marriage. "I pledge no new taxes." Wait a minute! What? What kind of pledge is that? A pledge signed by politicians to their political party is not a solid pledge because that political party does not elect them or keep them in office. A political pledge is between the voting constituents, the 99%, and the person running for office. Who in the world, running for office, would think about signing a pledge that ties the hands of their government? How is that a good idea? Don't you just love to see politicians when they are running for office? Do they inform the 99%, at that moment in time, that they are going to want their vote but not represent them? Who in the world, running for office, would think that the 99% and the 99% alone would be responsible for cleaning up the debt with no shared responsibility from the 1%? Signing a pledge of no new taxes makes that statement and if Republicans felt that way, why not campaign that way? United is in our title. People that are united share. Oh, my goodness, is the country heading for a divorce? Sure feels that way. Many Americans must feel used and abandoned because they voted for this 2010 group of non producing anything representatives. I feel fine, thank you for asking, because I did not vote for this mess of representatives and I did vote. I feel totally vindicated.

We know that politicians will never tell us their true thoughts and ideas. However, we must start insisting that we know the whole score. Do voters really want to elect someone into office who is more obligated to others than to them? Do voters want to elect someone into office who is taking orders from their political party and not from them? Well, guess what Republicans, these are your elected officials. Their loyalty is not to you, their voters. Their loyalty is not to their country, which is where they live. No, their loyalty is to their big bosses, their political party, whose only loyalty is to the 1%.

This "No new taxes ever" pledge originated from Grover Norquist, a lobbyist. Who in the world is Grover Norquist? He was not elected into any office. Why does he have such influence? This pledge states that no one can vote for an increase on taxes for the wealthy or big businesses EVER.[1] No matter how many seniors die because they can not get medical care, no new taxes. No matter how many children die from hunger, no new taxes. No matter how many women get cancer because of inadequate medical care, no new taxes. No matter how many disabled children can not get the facilities they need to make their lives livable, no new taxes. No matter how many of the elderly who need their meals from Meals on Wheels or their required prescriptions and can't get them, no new taxes. No matter how many bridges collapse and roads cave in, no new taxes. No matter how many schools are in disrepair, no new taxes. We must make cuts instead, more cuts, and more cuts, but no new taxes. No new revenue because it would be unjust to the 1% and that would be class warfare. No new revenue because Big Oil needs the subsidy. No new revenue because even though 83 out of 100 public corporations do not participate in the American economy by paying taxes,[2] those corporations need to keep their revenue, even if it is only to pay their CEO's and other managers big bonuses. No new revenue even though one day of tax cuts for millionaires equals feeding the needy for one year.[3]

There is the "Pro-Life Presidential Leadership" pledge, an anti-abortion pledge.[4] The originator of this pledge is the Susan B. Antony List group. Since Republicans repeatedly pass bill after bill about abortion, I guess this pledge was signed by all. There is a "Pro-marriage" pledge originating from The Family Leader.[5] This pledge is about politicians and their personal fidelity to their spouses and the respect for the marital bonds of others. Presidential hopeful Newt Gingrich signed this pledge and why not? He's been married three times and divorced twice so he is definitely pro-marriage. Then there is the "Cut, Cap, and Balance" pledge originating from a SuperPAC called Freedomworks.[6] This pledge is a Republican favorite and was a requirement for Republicans in Congress. It cuts spending to a lower level and caps it there for ten years. This pledge balances the budget without any added revenues. It's just another no taxes for the wealthy scheme. There is a "Lean Six Sigma" pledge which would eliminate spending deficits through waste reduction strategies, which translate into cutting middle class programs only.[7] I have no idea the originator of that pledge. Another pledge is the "Personhood" pledge by the Personhood organization.[8] This pledge was signed by all of the Republican presidential hopefuls and this pledge gives undeveloped zygotes full legal personhood rights. The purpose of this pledge is to ban abortions which is a Republican obsession. These pledges are all designed to force Republicans to adhere to advocacy groups and strange individuals, not the 99% voting them into office. These pledges eliminate any type of flexibility and any type of compromise. Hey, isn't that where we are now and why we are getting absolutely nothing accomplished in the year 2011?

It takes the majority of the 99% to elect an official who will only work for the 1%. Seems sort of backwards to me. Seems to me if a politician only has eyes for the 1%, then that politician should be recalled or not re-elected by the 99%. We don't get a lot from our politicians as it is but it would truly seem a waste of our vote to get absolutely nothing. When your politician pledges to never raise taxes on the wealthy, I think it is safe to say that you have a dud. You have an elected official who does not have any of your concerns on his to-do list. You are not his first agenda until it's election time, of course.

Just because we are the 99%, we deserve our own pledges. Let's pledge we will elect those who put our interest first. Let's pledge to elect only those who will work with any president for the good of the nation. Let's pledge to elect those who tell us they believe in shared sacrificing because we are one nation under God. Let's pledge to elect those who put the good of the nation first. Look at that, another short chapter and I did not even have to make a pledge.

Think of Something

The 99% loves to pretend that they can not figure out when they are being manipulated. The 99% refuses to think. Most of the lies presented to us are so unbelievable that it amazes me that anyone thinks they are plausible. I know that just because this President is black makes the unbelievable believable to those who hate this President and that capacity to fool themselves is scary. However, no matter how much the 99% does not want to think, our country demands it at this time in our history. Let's look at the ridiculous lies that Republicans keep telling the 99%. Let's think for just a second.

First lie is that there must not be any taxes on the wealthy and big businesses because the economy cannot grow with these increased taxes. Corporate taxes must be zero. Capital taxes must be zero. Inheritance taxes must be zero. Any tax on the wealthy must be as low as possible and as close to zero as possible. Let's just think about that for a minute. Times up! The problem with this logic is that the economy grew under the Clinton Administration and taxes were much higher than they are now. Not only did the economy grow, we ended President Clinton's Administration with a surplus. Doesn't President Clinton's approach to the economy sound like common sense? If we use the Republican's theory that the wealthy grow the economy with tax cuts, where was all of that growth with President George W Bush? We lost jobs for eight years and those tax cuts cost the American people $4 trillion. How does the 99% keep believing when history proves the lie? Taxes are at an all time low. We are not producing many jobs so tax cuts and no new revenue is not the answer to our problems.

Second lie is the only way out of this recession is spending cuts only. This idea rests on the theory that the only people who must bear the responsibility of debt reduction are those who have the least. The 1% must continue to receive their tax cuts and subsidies. Let's just think about that for a minute. Times up! Republicans have proposed to cut spending on programs that aid women, the elderly, and children, which would save approximately $110 million dollars a year.[1] However, the tax cuts for the wealthy will cost us $120 million dollars a day which will end up costing

$43 billion dollars a year.[2] $110 million a year as opposed to 43 billion a year. To make it even simpler, the proposed cuts of $110 million a year can be paid for with the $120 million a day of the wealthy tax cuts. Does that really require thinking about? Another example of this foolishness is the teachers and millionaires situation in Wisconsin. Remember when I was talking about the governors from hell and how they were trying to take amenities away from teachers and other public employees? Wisconsin Governor Scott wanted to take $5000 to $7000 from teachers salaries to balance his budget.[3] There are a little over 59,000 teachers in Wisconsin. However, there are almost 90,000 millionaires. Would a millionaire notice a lousy $5000 to $7000 dip in their salary? Wouldn't it have been better to take a small amount from those who have the most as oppose to taking a large amount from those who have so little? Every Republican's plan for anything always involves some type of spending cut for the 99% while keeping tax breaks or subsidies for the 1%. Congress is especially fond of farm subsidies because as I have stated previously, many families of congressional members are getting those subsidies. 62% of American farms do not get any subsidies however, six Democrats and their farming families received a total of $489,856. Now, you know Republicans can do better than that. Seventeen Republicans and their farming families received a total of $5,334,565.[4] Wow, that is impressive from a group of people who want the 99% to anti up on everything. 74% of these farm subsidies go to the largest and wealthiest 10% of farms. Oh Congress, I just found huge savings for the country and none of the 99% is affected. Ha-ha, I was just kidding because we all know that the 99% is not the concern of Congress.

Third lie is the Health Care Bill will bankrupt the United States because it just cost too much. Let's just think about that for a minute. Times up! Doing nothing in healthcare will bankrupt the United States because the Federal Government pays for the uninsured. Denying the 99% affordable healthcare will bankrupt and kill Americans. Trying to kill Medicare will bankrupted and kill Americans. The Congressional Budget Office (CBO) concluded that the new Healthcare Law's impact would actually reduce the deficit because new taxes would offset the cost.[5] Repealing would actually add to the deficit. Who knows if the CBO has the correct figures or not because the issue is not the figures. It's about the people who do not have health insurance. What are Republicans trying to do to this country and to the 99%? Does anyone see the pattern in all of this? Surely I don't have to think this through for the 99% because even this lie is as easy to decipher as the true death panel, which is the Ryan budget plan. No matter how much we are told that the Ryan bill will not kill Medicare, it will. Those of us in traditional Medicare would see our premiums rise as fewer people remain in the risk pool to share the costs of the program. We would not be able to afford Medicare and that is what will kill it. No matter how much we are told that this is just a liberal spin, it is not. No matter how many charts are presented, no matter how many graphs are shown, no matter how many Republicans back this budget plan, this plan will bankrupt the United States and kill grandma.[6] The Ryan Plan, which is endorsed by most Republicans in Washington, will take years to implement with years of living poorly for most of the 99%. This plan proposes $4.3 trillion in cuts to programs for the needy and $4.2 trillion in tax cuts to the wealthy. This is in no way a debt reduction plan, as advertised. This is a plan that requires no revenue from the 1%, no shared sacrifice, just pain for the needy and windfalls for the 1%. This plan rests solely on the backs of the 99%. The only healthcare initiative that Republicans seem galvanized about is the issue of abortion. They appear to be using women reproductive rights to try and avoid any jobs bill. On October 13, 2011, the House passed another bill restricting women on abortion even if it is a health issue. The bill was appropriately called "Women will die" Bill.[7] So, I ask once again, why are women backing a party that does not care about their health in any form? Republicans want women with child but with no healthcare for that woman or child. That is absolutely priceless.

Fourth lie is that the President is taking the country in the wrong direction. Polls show that over half of the 99% think we are heading in the wrong direction.[8] Let's just think about that for a minute. Times up! I ask only one question of those who feel the President is taking us in the wrong direction. When did we start going in the wrong direction? The President had reversed our job losses to job gains by 2010.[9] The 99% decided to reverse those gains by adding more "NO" Republicans to the mix. That would be the 2010 Republicans who promised jobs. Those same 2010 Republicans have voted against every jobs bill presented by Democrats. Those same 2010 Republicans have voted and delayed the President's Jobs Bill. Those same 2010 Republicans have produced no jobs bill just recycled ideas that rarely produce jobs. Those same 2010 Republicans, who keep telling the 99% that the President is taking the country in the wrong direction, are those same 2010 Republicans who refuse to vote on anything that will benefit the country. This lie proves my allegation of racism because there is no way that anyone can believe that Republicans, whose policies are responsible for this economic situation that we are in, know the correct way to take the country. There is no evidence that cutting programs for the poor and giving tax cuts to the wealthy will take our country in the right direction. There is no evidence that any of the old tried and failed polices that Republicans are pushing at Americans will ever work. The only evidence that we have of the country going in the wrong direction is the Bush Administration. To give President Obama one year and 10 months to correct eight years of deregulated policies, tax cuts, loopholes, and unpaid for programs and wars along with a collapsing financial system is unconscionable. Just say you do not like black people and save us all this crap about the country going in the wrong direction. I will respect people more for their honesty.

Fifth big lie is that the President does not show any leadership. This is something I hear a lot because this allegation is necessary to keep the 99% thinking we are going the wrong way. Democrats are even ducking the President because they are afraid that the allegation will stick to them also. It does not come as shock to me because I have always said that this President is in this fight for the 99% alone. So, let's just think about that for a minute. Times up! Amazingly, this President has no problem with leadership around the world. He was able to catch the worst terrorists and improve the world's opinion about us. He was able to give us affordable healthcare, $20 billion escrow for an oil spill, protect us with the Consumer Protection Agency, withdraw the troops from Iraq, and still have time to enact the largest reform for student aid in 40 years. He rescued the auto industry and helped us with his economic stimulus plan. He has even performed Congress's job and submitted a jobs bill. The President even purchased fuel efficient American made cars for the government's fleet of cars. Anyone truly interested in witnessing true leadership only has to go to the Obama Achievement Center and be blown away with what this President has accomplished with Republicans working against him on everything.[10] The 99% tied this President's hands behind his back, with the election of a bevy of "NO" politicians, who would vote against their mothers rather than work with this President on anything. Americans elected the chaos and they need to admit to their culpability in this fiasco. Show me anyone who can lead a crowd whose only concern is to get you voted out of office at the cost of everything. Show me anyone who can get bills passed with a crowd who votes down their own bills. Show me anyone who can make compromises with a crowd who will not ever compromise. Show me this leader because he does not exist. The 99% knows this but once again there is this constant need to use anything to have a reason to dislike this President. I refuse to applaud this foolishness. I hope for the best for the 99%, but then I hoped for the best just before the 2010 midterm elections and look how that turned out. The 99% brought this political mess on themselves and there is no way that they can lay this in the President's lap, no way. The 99% put the President's hands in cement and then tries to pretend that he is not a leader. I am getting mad and pretty soon I will have to start calling names. I will have to call Americans lazy and stupid. Ooh, that's right, I have already done that many times. My bad!

Final big lie is that the President and the President alone is responsible for job creation. Let's just think about that for a minute. Times up! As I said before and I said in "Jobs, What Jobs," jobs are created in the states. Corporations and small businesses operate in states not in Washington D.C. States are responsible for 150 million or more jobs while the Federal Government only employs two million.[11] The President is not responsible for writing a bill to create jobs. Yes, he can give suggestion. Yes, he can plead for the people. Yes, he can use whatever influence he has and the bully pulpit to make whatever difference he can, but he can not make Congress pass any bill. That responsibility is on Congress and Congress alone. For the 99% to allow themselves to be hoodwinked into thinking anything else proves my claim of people wanting the President to fail. If this is the criteria that many Americans will use to help this President become a one-term President, then so be it. However, when the joblessness does not improve, when you have the governors from hell, more politicians who do not care, and the crazies calling the shots, do not, I repeat, do not complain. Take it like the good complacent 99% who keeps believing the manipulators. What makes all of this especially funny is how Republicans and FOX News convinced the 99% that the President was responsible for a jobs bill in 2011. Didn't Americans elect all of those Republicans in 2010 because they promised jobs? Where was the Republican's jobs bill at the beginning of 2011 or 2012? Where was the demanding 99% making Republicans produce jobs or at least a jobs bill? Instead we hear that both sides are responsible. The 99% took that responsibility away from the President. They voted massively for those who told them they would produce jobs and made no effort to stand by their promise.

Just because we are the 99%, we must question all of this misinformation and realize that it is not beneficial in any way to the 99%. Surely, just because the President is black would not make voters that crazy, would it? Let's just think about that for a minute. Times up! Let's think about the way we are being laughed at because of our capacity to be manipulated into the destruction of ourselves. As perplexing as this all seems, this is where America is at this time in history with a Black President. Let's think about our children and how disappointed they will be if their fathers and mothers allow the complete destruction of their nation. Let's think about how long this recession with be for the 99%. Let's think about how easily we could have been on the road to recovery if we had not diverted our attention in 2010. Let's think about how we are 100% responsible and will be for quite some time. Let's think about all of these things but whatever happens let's just try to think. Times up!

ALL MY CHILDREN

Something happened in 2009. Some of our elected officials changed from esteemed representatives to people who you can't bring home to Mama. Despite the US current economic situation, President Obama has been saddle with a childish legislature that is directly responsible for our slow recovery. How many times has President Obama tried to shame Congress into doing anything? At his news conference on June 20th, he stated that Malia and Sasha took care of their homework a day early and did not wait until the last minute. My favorite comment was that Malia and Sasha don't do all nighters.[1] I laughed because I understood exactly what he was saying. Congress works two weeks and then takes two weeks off.[2] The House is off while the Senate is in session and then the Senate is off while the House is in session. Seriously, how can anything get done? Our government stays in limbo on bill after bill and no one admits to the deceptive maneuvers to sabotage the President's agenda. The President keeps asking Congress to act like the adults that they are and no matter what he says, nothing gets through. Just because the President is black means Republicans can act as ugly as they want because they hate the fact that this President is superior to them. That's right, I said it. President Obama is superior to all those Republicans because he puts the 99% first. He puts our needs and our agenda first. He acts like what we want in our government. He acts like the adult in the room.

The President has been in office for three years and he still has judicial nominees and department heads still in limbo. What is causing the delay? Could it be Republican's childish maneuvers to deny the President any of his agenda? President Obama felt that the Federal Courts should look like America. He felt that we should all be included in this democracy. However, his judicial selections have been held up longer than any other president. The trumped up reasoning is that when you try to create diversity, you lower your standards.[3] Let me see if I understand this reasoning. If a black man, a Hispanic man, or a woman is selected, the standards have been lowered. The fact, that all of those groups have been discriminated against for years to keep them out of those positions, does not seem to enter into the picture. The fact, that the President did not lower his standards but just eliminated discriminatory barriers thus casting a wider net, would never occur to the naysayers. Congress should treat this President with the respect that he deserves and that means respecting his decisions for his department heads and judicial choices. The 99% must insist that Congress stop acting like children and perform their duties as our elected officials. Ha-ha, that was a good one. I'm so crazy.

How many times can the Republican legislators show us their childish behavior. We saw that behavior with the debt ceiling debate. The President offered the Republicans a four to one deal. $4 trillion in spending cuts to $1 trillion in revenue and their response was "No."[4] The government would default and the Republicans said "No." The Republicans stomped their feet and got their way. We saw that behavior with the extension of unemployment. We saw that behavior with the potential government shutdown. We keep seeing this behavior and we keep taking polls. Our polls show Congress with an 13% rating and still the childish behavior continues.[5] We learn as children that there are repercussions for bad behavior. That is not the case with our Congressional representatives. When will the 99% insist on mutual respect and cooperation?

Since the day that President Obama entered office, there has been an extreme level of disrespect. What are we teaching our children with this denigrating behavior? We watched as South Carolina Representative Joe Wilson shouted "You lie" when the President was giving a Healthcare Speech.[6] We saw Louisiana Representative Jeff Landry holding a home made sign saying "Drilling equals jobs."[7] We watched as Georgia Representative Paul Brown refuse to attend the President's State of the Union address opting to tweet in his office instead. Illinois Representative Joe Walsh decided to just read the text of the speech rather than attend in person. There is always some Republican boycotting the President's speeches just so that everyone can see their distaste for this President.[8] We have seen House Majority Leader Eric Cantor and others texting while the President is addressing them in the chamber.[9] We heard Colorado Representative Doug Lamborn's statement that he did not want to associate with Obama because it was like touching a tar baby.[10] We witnessed Speaker of the House John Boehner and Representative Eric Cantor walking out on the debt ceiling meeting with the President.[11] Speaker Boehner even refused the date the President requested for his Jobs Bill speech and he became the first Speaker in American history to refuse a president's request.[12] Republicans refuse to treat Barack Obama with the deference due the President of the United States. The 99% has allowed this behavior. The 99% has not insisted on respect in our government. There can never be any type of compromise if people can not respect each other in their dealings with each other.

What ever happened to the conservative request that we show the President respect when we are at war? Hasn't President Obama been at war his entire term? Sean Hannity of FOX News said we should not undermine a Commander-in-Chief while we are at war. Bill O'Reilly said "You don't criticize the Commander-in-Chief in the middle of a firefight. That would be construed as putting US forces in jeopardy and undermining morale."[13] Where are those voices now at this time of our history. Oh, that right, those comments were for President Bush, who started the wars. I guess the second recipient of those wars does not get the same consideration. Oh 99%, where are you? By any chance are you seeing this disruptive pattern of lies and manipulation?

When the President is the First Black, everything changes. Disrespect is allowed. Duplicity is allowed. Actually, everything is allowed because this President must fail. Unfortunately, that means the 99% will also fail. The correct way to handle the first in anything is for everyone to participate. The 99% must elect those who can work for our nation with respect for each other. It will not work any other way. We must elect those who want change and not those who want to repeat their old failed policies. We did not do that in 2010. In our rush to punish this President and believe everything that was thrown at us, we elected those who would throw tantrums and leave us in a recession rather than cooperate and work for solutions. We are witnessing extremely bad behavior and the 99% has allowed all of it. With that 2010 vote, we left the President alone to deal with the most obstinate, childish, and misbehaving people. Over and over again they informed us that they would not work with the new President. On top of that, their racism resulted in the highest level of disrespect ever witnessed. Really, is that any way to treat the new kid on the block? Is that any way to act like the adults in the voting booth? It's out fault. I keep bringing this up again and again because as a Nana, it is my duty to be repetitive. However, even with all of this disrespect and childish behavior, this President always smiles and shows his respect for everyone. This President is succeeding and hopefully the 99% is aware.

Just because we are the 99%, we can not keep being the Erica Cain in this relationship. Calm down, I will explain. Erica Cain on the soap opera "All My Children" married several husbands but she always remained Erica Cain. She never changed and got better. She just stayed the same old selfish, I want my way on everything, Erica Cain. This is where we are at this time in our history. We think we still have two parties working for our nation. That is not true because race has entered the picture, attitudes have changed, and Republicans have gone to the dark side (giggles). Acting childish does not affect them because there are no repercussions. Polls do not affect them because they know that the electorate will keep them in office because of party loyalty and now because of race. We tied the President's hands with the election of 2010. We claimed that we wanted more bipartisanship, even though we witnessed the President's constant attempts for compromise and the constant rejection. The President has been the adult and Congress has acted like angry children. The President is too nice to blame the 99% for their own demise. Luckily, I am not a nice Nana. I am a realist. We are where we are because of how the 99% voted. We handicapped the President. He does not cave, we eliminated his choices. We must accept responsibility for our actions, take the blame, and make better choices. If we can not get beyond race and stop believing the lies, then the 99% can expect nothing for a very long time. The 99% will have just shown all of our children the foolishness of our ways and our racists decisions. This is all about the children and their seeing our racism. This is all about the children and how they will become the new 99% who must live with diversity in a global economy. The 99% must start being the shining example for all the children.

WE VOTED FOR THAT

(NOT ME)

We, the 99%, have been hoodwinked worst than the Indians at Thanksgiving. While Republicans are convincing the 99% to ditch this President, they are making changes to ensure that they keep control whether we vote their way or not. Misinformation has been working for Republicans for quite a while. However, sometimes, people detect the lies and react. Sometimes people think and make good decisions. Granted, we have not made good decisions recently but there is always hope for the future. At some point, the 99% will not want to be ruled by the 1%. At some point, the 99% will want a strong and prosperous middle class again. At some point, the 99% will want better pay and nicer homes. That will not be our future if the 1% continues to control our politicians. Once Republicans see that we have suffered enough, they know we will want to reverse their policies. Therefore, they have placed priorities on implementing changes that will ensure that our votes are compromised permanently.

First change that Republicans are making is trying to decimate unions, which they perceive to be the Democratic base.[1] Collective bargaining has been impacted. Pensions and healthcare initiatives are in jeopardy. Those seeking better pay and better working conditions, unions, are losing their clout.[2] Right to Work is now becoming a de facto standard resulting in lower salaries and fewer pensions. Teachers are laid off and policemen are furloughed. Republicans governors claim that state deficits are because of unions while they give away millions in taxpayers money to campaign donating corporations in the form of subsidies.[3] Who will protect the 99% in the work environment? Unions let down their guard, trusted Republicans, and placed a whole bunch of Republicans in office in 2010. The part about trusting was the most egregious and embarrassing for the unions. Unions are really angry now because they realize they were duped. I don't understand how they thought Republicans, who always professed their hatred for them, had changed. However, the real question will be how much will the 99% suffer because they have no group to work for better wages, higher and better working standards, and all of the benefits that unions painstakingly worked to achieve? Well, what ever happens, we voted for that.

Second change that Republicans are making involves voting rules.[4] The new voting rules eliminate some of the early voting days and requires a photo ID. The reason early voting was targeted was because usually old people, poor people, and young people vote early.[5] Old people vote early because they can not stand a long time and they need to be at the restaurant in time for the Early Bird special. Poor people vote early because they have to work on Tuesday, which is traditionally voting day. If the bus is late or if after picking up their children they are behind schedule, then they miss the vote. Young people vote early because they are young and have things to do. All three of those groups, traditionally, vote Democratic and they really turned out for President Obama in the 2008 election. Thus, Republicans needed to eliminate as much early voting as possible. Republicans also changed the rules so that everyone would need a photo ID to vote. Now, this is not a bad idea, it's just an inconvenient idea. Republicans threw in the photo ID to eliminate those who do not have a photo ID, which would include a lot of old people, poor people, and young people. Wow, those three groups are taking a beating from Republicans. However, we voted for that.

Third change that Republicans are making involves redistricting and this is the most insidious of all. When governors and legislatures are allowed to draw up districts that only benefit their party, that is un-American. We are suppose to be a nation that votes our officials into office by a majority. However, with our 2010 votes flooding our states and legislatures with Republicans, we have truly created a monster which we may never recover. The best examples of manipulating the districts are in Florida, Arizona, and Texas, of course. Floridians voted for two amendments and those two amendments were for fair redistricting. Every since we voted for those amendments, our Republican legislature has been trying to find a way around those amendments. They have tried to manipulate the software. They have had public meetings, for voter input, without maps of any of the districts. They have removed the compactness and geospatial analysis from the software and are instructed to answer no questions about this analysis.[6] Voters did not vote for this type of slick maneuver and apparently many are not even aware of what their legislature is trying to do to them. This is classic voter suppression through manipulation of the districts and Floridians, like the rest of the 99%, will never see it coming. Arizona is playing the same Floridian game of manipulating their redistricting. Eleven years ago, Arizona voters handed their redistricting over to an independent commission, instead of its legislature.[7] Their reasoning was that neither party might play fair. In November 2011, Republican Governor Jan Brewer convened the Senate to remove the head of the Redistricting Commission because she did not like their redistricting plan. This Governor and her legislature are in the process of usurping the will of the voters. Governor Rick Perry of Texas also signed a new redistricting map. A Justice Department lawyer stated there was ample circumstantial evidence of the intent to limit the voting rights of Hispanics, which is a violation of the Voting Rights Act. This redistricting plan would affect nearly 500,000 Hispanics.[8] Redistricting seems to be the way that parities will manipulate our vote and our democracy. When I see so many Republicans elected to office, with their idiotic ideas, it makes me wonder how long we have been duped by this redistricting. Like I said before, Rick Scott did become the Governor of Florida (giggles) and we voted for that.

Fourth change that Republicans want is changes to the Electoral College in some states. This would only be the states that a Democrat might carry.[9] Here is the gist of this issue. Most states are winner takes all.[10] Nebraska splits their electoral votes. Nebraska voted Republican except for one stray electoral vote for Barack Obama. Republicans want that split vote eliminated. However, in states that traditionally vote for Democrats, Republicans want split electoral votes.[11] Does everyone understand what this is all about? If Republican states can have winner takes all electoral votes and Democratic states have split electoral votes, there is no way a Democrat will ever win the presidency, ever. Whatever the Republican agenda is will be what this nation will become. That is another one of the gifts from the 2010 midterm elections. We elected our permanent masters but we voted for that.

Finally, we must thwart the middle class hating Supreme Court with their Citizen United ruling. That ruling stated that corporations, unions, and any other hidden organization can spend billions on advertisements for or against a candidate running for office.[12] This ruling destroyed our campaign finance laws. This ruling made it more difficult for us to hold anyone accountable for the lies told. So, we as citizens must take the matter into our own hands. If we see an advertisement for or against a candidate and that advertisement does not end with the candidate saying "And I approve this message," then we ignore that message. If the candidate knows that the advertisement is true, then he has to own that message. Remember when John McCain and his campaign were insinuating that Barack Obama was an Arab? John McCain allowed the misinformation to continue until a little old lady informed him that she could not vote for Barack Obama because he was an Arab.[13] John McCain then had to publicly disavow the message and he looked foolish for allowing the lie. We did not vote for this directly however, we voted for previous presidents who selected these Supreme Court Justices who are following their political agenda instead of following the law.

Just because we are the 99%, we have allowed Republicans to think they have a true mandate. We have really stepped in it this time. Usually we can convince ourselves that we did not cause our own suffering. However, this time it is too obvious. We can not deny the direct results of our foolishness in the 2010 election. Since most of the 99% are blamers by nature and since the President is black by heredity, everyone had their perfect scapegoat. However, let's not get it twisted. The cause of all of our problems are on the 99% because we are the majority. Blame the President until the sky falls, which I hear is real soon. Blame Democrats, blame your children, blame your dog or your cat, blame anyone and anything that makes your idiotic behavior palpable. It really does not matter who you blame or believe because the decisions of the 2010 midterm elections changed America. Therefore, that leaves me with only one thing to say. We voted for that (not me).

AND SO IT GOES

There are many examples of what to never do again but none has the impact of Wisconsin. It is also a perfect example of what our government will look like in a couple of years of Republican rule. After taking their well tuned government and dumping it upside down, the people of Wisconsin are trying to recover. Wisconsin tried to recall some of their elected representatives, as I have suggested throughout this book, and they lost by one seat. The district where they lost was the same district that came up with 7000 mysterious votes to boost a Wisconsin conservative Supreme Court Justice into office in a very close election.[1] Maybe it's time we put Federal Marshals in Wisconsin voting districts and make everyone put ink on their hands, like any other third world country.

The 99% had better wake up and understand that they are under attack and that was proven to all with the recalls in Wisconsin. As soon as the middle class showed their discontent of the assault on them and tried to democratically recall those who did not have the welfare of the 99%, big money rolled in. There was so much hidden big money spent in Wisconsin for the recall that they set a record for the entire nation.[2] Why would so much big money enter this race? The message was simple and that message was that big money is in charge. Our democracy is about to become a plutocracy or an oligarchy. A plutocracy is governance by the wealthy and an oligarchy is governance by a small group of people. Wait a minute! Isn't that what we have already? Isn't money determining races? Why is the 99% allowing, note I said allowing, themselves to be divided to the point of having absolutely no control. Wisconsin has only 1% of their population that makes over $250,000.[3] How in the world are the wealthy controlling that state? Is the 99% so foolish as to believe what big money tells them? It is embarrassing to see people cater to the lies from big money. Many Wisconsin politicians are disciples of big bucks, aka, the Kock Brothers.[4]

It's so embarrassing to see people believe the lies about the teachers who teach their children just because big money and FOX News tells them to believe. It's so embarrassing to watch this spectacle take place and many people pretend to not understand this type of manipulation. Most of the 99% should know enough teachers to know that these are vicious lies and meant to try and eliminate teacher's unions. If the 99% can try and make the effort to understand these attempts to discredit teachers then they should be able to understand the manipulations and lies about President Obama. Why do many of the 99% keep hanging onto the misinformation? Why is the 99% pretending that all of this discord is anything other that racism?

Just because we are the 99%, we forgot our responsibility. We assumed that our democracy would always stay intact. We assumed that a little misinformation would not harm us. We assumed we could nudge our economy with a quick fix. We missed the mark by a quite a lot and now we have to repair the damage. However, we cannot repair anything if we are not a solid 99%. Okay, that's probably not doable so let's just go for 52%. If not, this country will deserve Republicans. This country will deserve to be like Wisconsin, where their rights are being taken away day by day. This country will deserve to be like Michigan, where the elected officials are usurped by their governor. This country will deserve to be like Florida, where any minute now we will have to be drug tested to vote. Oops, I do not want to give the governors from hell any ideas because from my lips to their agenda and so it goes.

It's Racism, Seriously

When President Obama was elected to office, many people thought that we had turn the corner on racism. Black Americans,12% of the 99%, knew that it was not true. The 12% knew, with a little time, we would see the real reaction to the first Black President. The 12% knew that there would be snide comments with racial overtones. The 12% knew that southern congressional representatives would be resistant. However, no one expected an entire party to go to the dark side (giggles). So, let's quickly recap how we got to where we are in 2011.

For eight years, President Bush and Republicans manipulated the economy for their agenda. President Clinton gave President Bush a $300 billion surplus and President Bush gave President Obama a $14 trillion deficit. Apparently, from 2000-2008, Republicans did not pay for anything. They gave two huge tax cuts to their buddies, the 1%, and never made any offsets. Now, they are screaming for offsets on everything. They did not pay for the wars, though they did find money for quite a few of the 1% like Halliburton and other contractors.[1] Now, they want spending cuts from the 99% only. They did not pay for the prescription part of Medicare, though it was used by many seniors. Now, they want to kill Medicare. They did not pay for "No Child Left Behind." Now they want to cut education and teachers. They deregulated and ignored security alerts and we ended up with the Gulf Oil spill and 9/11, just to name a few. Finally in 2008, because of all of the deregulation, banks and other financial institutions started to fail. We ended President Bush's eight years in office with a financial meltdown, record unemployment, and a deficit of $14 trillion.

With much excitement, we elected President Obama expecting hope and change. Instead we got dissension, misinformation, and racism. I expected racism. I just thought that the 99% would admit to it and react against it. Unfortunately, that is not what has happened. How do I know this? Because of the election of 2010. That is my shinning example of "It's racism, seriously."

President Obama was sworn into office in January 2009. The Tea Party, which was haled as the real Americans, started in February 2009.

President Obama had not enacted one policy and already there was a group claiming he was taking the county in the wrong direction. There were all kinds of divisive rhetoric and insulting posters for this President. The proof of racism was there for all to see but the 99% pretended that the Tea Party was just angry Americans. The President was blamed for TARP, even though it started in 2008. He was blamed for the rising unemployment, even though it had been rising since 2000. However, the most racist actions of all were the Congressional Republicans and their refusal to work and clean up the financial disaster that they left for this President. The 99% watched this all transpire and decided that it was not racist, just political bantering. As the unemployment continued to rise from the policies of the Bush Administration, the 99% was being whipped into a frenzy with the divisive rhetoric from the Tea Party, Republicans, and FOX News. The 99% did not know that the Tea Party was being funded by the 1%. As our deficit continued to rise from the policies and tax cuts from the Bush Administration, the 99% was being misinformed as to who was the responsible parties.

All of these antics were divide and conquer maneuvers that have worked for centuries. Kings and Queens used these antics along with dictators and democracies. When Republicans refused to participate in the recovery of our nation, many talking heads said that they were never going to be elected into anything again because the 99% would punish them for their inactivity. I hoped they were true but I suspected that we were all going to get the usual "It's not racism." line. The 99% refused to label any of Republican's actions as racist. The fact that they voted against their own bills did not ring a bell. The fact that they said "NO" on everything did not ring a bell. The fact that they showed so much disrespect did not ring a bell. The 99% pretended and denied racism, which all led to the 2010 midterm elections.

After eight years of financial foolishness, two and ten months of refusing to help the nation, the 99% performed as expected and returned Republicans back into a position of power in the 2010 midterm elections. They could not sweep the Senate but the House was a piece of cake. The 99% had already been whipped into a frenzy over House Speaker Nancy Pelosi. So, the misinformation was working beautifully. With the Tea Party anger and Republicans and FOX News misinformation, the 99%, with their constant denial, never had a chance.

Placing congressional Republicans back into power was a foolish move and all of the gridlock and chaos is the proof. The blame goes solely to the 99%, those who voted and those who refused to vote. However, those congressional Republicans could only affect us on a national level. The election of Republican governors and filling our state legislatures with so many Republicans, so much so that they had a super majority, was the most foolish and racist action of all. The 99% refused to see racism in any of their actions and now, for once, they get to live the life on the other end of racism.

The 2010 midterm elections showed the Republicans the key to success. They have their success in the states with Republican governors and their legislatures as they go after the rights of unions, change voting rules, redistrict, and change the Electoral College. They have their success as they stall on job creation initiatives They have their success as they try and manipulate the Consumer Protection Agency, FAA, Post Office, and EPA. Republicans have their success as they blame the President for every negative action they bring on this nation. They have their success because of their racist attitude and the 99% showing them that they are okay with their actions. For all those who have said over and over again that this is not about race, wake up! The 99% is about to lose their country over their inability to admit to racism. Stop the denial.

Just because we are the 99%, we must be participants by voting people into office to help our government function for our basic needs. If we make the right selection, we can sit back and relax. If we make the right selection, our rights are always protected. If we make the right selection, we remain the best democracy. If, If, If, and I still have property in the Everglades. Hate can not be the determining factor for the IF's in our lives. We can not allow the crazies and their hate message to destroy our way of life. There is no way that the 99% can pretend they do not see this racism. I'll bet your children see it. I'll bet your children are watching you like a hawk and trying to figure why you are lying to yourself. I'll bet your children are wondering why you are tripping over this remarkable new President who they really like a lot. I'll bet you are looking like a disappointment to them. I'll bet if you ask them, they will tell you "Yes Mom, or Dad, it's racism, seriously.

Turning in the Right Direction

Hopefully by now, we realize we didn't get what we voted for in the 2010 midterm elections. Since we cannot recall this current batch of politicians and apparently we can't stop them from their foolish behavior, we must take it upon ourselves to move the country in the right direction. To accomplish this, we need to ask the right questions and hold politicians accountable for the answers that will take us in the right direction. We are so divided we can not see the forest for the trees. We only see conservatives and liberals and Democrats and Republicans, the trees. We never see our nation, the forest. We are under attack at this moment in time. We are at war with those who want our country under their thumbs with the 99% having no rights and very few privileges. We are not asking the right questions and demanding solutions.

1. How do we, the 99%, get our jobs back? We must buy "Made in America." We must show companies that they can only have us as consumers if they create jobs in America. We keep it simple. As mentioned before, if we buy 50% of your product, you owe us at least 50% of the jobs manufacturing of that product. This is a quick method that will produce rapid results. Since some companies have shifted all of their jobs overseas, then our boycott of their products will not affect any American jobs. A win-win for the 99%. Like I said before, the 99% buys more crap than any other nation and we buy two and three pieces of that crap (giggles). Therefore, the 99%, must take charge of its future with its purchase power. Unfortunately, manufacturing alone will not be enough. President Obama has initiated several innovative tools, for jobs of the future, so that our nation can make strides for that future.[1] Since the young people of our nation are a significant portion of the unemployed,[2] our high schools and colleges must create programs, in conjunction with the Federal Government, that will help their

graduates prepare for these different types of jobs. Curriculums must change. Areas where innovation will benefit our economy are training tools for retrofitting our country for energy efficiency, careers utilizing innovative ideas for other energy sources in our economy, e-commerce, and innovative healthcare options. We need jobs but we must create opportunities for the future growth of our nation.

2. How do we, the 99%, persuade our banks to participate in our economic recovery? We start moving our money to banks who are willing to loan businesses money to assist in job creation. The banks caved when we objected to their ATM fee so we know they are being attentive. Banks must employ the regulations that they were using before they accrued their toxic assets so that they can start lending again. We must insist that banks stop foreclosures, now. Here is the gist of foreclosures. One or two is not significant, but when entire neighborhoods are affected, then a change has to occur. Instead of banks foreclosing, readjust the monthly mortgage to the present cost of the house. It is always better to have someone paying something on a house than that house sitting empty and being vandalized. No one should accept a foreclosure notice without the banks showing them the proper paperwork which will be very difficult for many banks.[3] Everyone must participate in our recovery especially those who were bailed out.

3. How do we, the 99%, change our economy for the future? We only have to work on three things. (Wow, really!) That would be our tax code, our housing situation, and our trade deals. Our tax code must be fairer for the working 99%. The 1% has benefited from this inequality in our tax code and now they must contribute so that we can reduce the deficit without cutting the 99% programs. If our tax rate is 29%, then that is the minimum tax rate for the 1%. Actually, the rates were higher under President Clinton and we should return to those rates because we ended with a surplus. We must insist on the housing situation being modified so that those who are under water can still live in their homes. Banks must work with the Federal Government so that homeowners are given relief. This allows those homeowners to become consumers again. We must insist that our trade deals are made fairer so that everyone benefits and we are not forever behind the eight ball. If that means

that we should use businessmen to help in the negotiations, so be it. We must make sure we only elect those congressmen who will broker trade deals that are job creators and are beneficial to the 99%.

4. How do we, the 99%, clean up politics? The 99% must end corporate control of our politicians. Congress must enact an amendment that overturns the Citizen United ruling by our middle class hating Supreme Court. We must acknowledge and prevent the influence that money currently has on our elections. Before any election, local television stations and newspapers must offer reduce rates with a few freebies for advertisements. All advertisements must end with "And I approve this message." This will eliminate outside influences (SuperPACs, etc)from trying to manipulate our choices. The cost of running for office can be reduced by having town meetings and debates with all the candidates. All local newspapers and television stations must be our fact checkers for all political claims. Once elected, our representatives must email their constituents about all bills and how that bill will impact them. If the governors from hell are an indicator of our future, we must change the recall laws. Nineteen states have recall of state officials and all states must have that ability. Anyone can make a mistake and we must be able to rectify our moment of foolishness. Our voting laws must not be altered so that we restrict the ability of anyone to vote. Redistricting must be achieved by a non-biased committee which we, the 99%, select, not our bias legislature. All elections must be transparent and provable. Here is an easy way to decide who should be in office. Any person running for office, who wants restrictions on voting, is against recall overhaul, is putting Emergency Managers in towns and cities, is trying to dilute the 99% from joining unions, pushes an agenda to restrict women health and productive rights, and is not in favor of all Americans sharing in the recovery of this country, should not be considered for office. 99%, you are so welcome (giggles).

5. How do we, the 99%, clean up Wall Street and the greed of the 1%? First we need economic justice which means our financial criminals need to be imprisoned along with monetary punishment. Congress must address our tax code so that tax evasion and tax loopholes are eliminated. Congress can pass sensible laws that protect the 99% from shady dealings by banks, corporations, lending services,

and hedge fund operators. We enhance the Consumer Protection Agency to have the power to advertise truthfully about those who are trying to manipulate us as consumers. We get rid of duplicate laws that are not beneficial to the 99%. We all know the saying, "To much is given, much is expected." Sorry about that 1%, but over the years, your wealth has increased substantially. You must help in this recovery by hiring since you have been pegged as the job creators. Since small businesses are the heart and soul of this country, our government must continue to invest more in those businesses and trim down subsidies to the huge conglomerates so that everyone can have a piece of the pie.

6. How do we, the 99%, get shared sacrificing? We have asked nicely, now we have to change laws. There must be a new tax code with mandatory percentage rates. No one can earn millions and not pay any taxes. There must be a base tax on all incomes and investments. Adjustments can be made only to a certain extent. Tax havens and tax loopholes must be eliminated. Subsidies can be given to businesses that are new and need assistance but those subsidies must be monitored and eliminated when they are not needed any longer. If a company, like the oil companies, is making millions in profit, then those subsidies are no longer needed and can be used elsewhere. Since one day of the tax cuts for the 1% can fund one of our programs, eliminate the tax cuts and we have 365 programs fully funded.

7. How do we, the 99%, get from under so much debt? The 99% must act financially responsible going forward. For example, if you make $50,000, you can not afford a mortgage on a $500,000 house. We need a Mortgage App. We put in our salary and the App figures what price home we can afford. This will eliminate the banks duping us again. We will also have to make cuts to our favorite programs and if we are very careful, we can eliminate most of the waste and duplication of services. This will create savings while continuing services that benefit the 99%. If our Affordable Healthcare needs to be amended so that the cost is less or the service is better, we encourage our representative to amend, not repeal. The 99% needs healthcare and we should not elect anyone who is repealing and not improving. Privatization is a rip off. Contracting out to smaller independent companies is better because everyone is benefiting.

Medicare needs an overhaul but it must not be eliminated because it is a staple for many seniors. The same goes for Social Security. We make whatever cost effective changes we can make and clean up the waste. No country should allow its seniors or less fortunate to live in poverty while the 1% does not share in the recovery.

8. How do we, the 99%, educate our children and keep them safe in the process? The Federal Government would have the responsibility to enact standards that all states must adhere to. All children must be able to read by grade two. That standard would be the most significant because reading is fundamental to the entire experience of being educated. This reading standard would not be simple "See Spot Run" books, it would be 100 page children books which would be read in class by every student. Every state's format for "A" schools is right there for all to follow. No federal money for private schools. Give senior citizens free lunch at schools and they can be the school's security force or really just their lookouts for bullies. Any bullying is addressed immediately. School lunches will be local and as fresh as possible. Physical Education will be reinstated in all schools. Since sport billionaire owners like to have lockouts about their excess money, the billionaires can contribute part of their revenues to schools for sports equipment. We will even name the gymnasium after those owners. There must be some type of debt forgiveness for college students who intern with federal programs. There must be some type of loan relief so that graduates can become consumers.

9. How do we, the 99%, ensure that in the future partisan politics does not overshadow the true democratic process from taking place? The only agenda of our elected officials should be improvement for the 99%. Therefore we recall and send politicians home. We do not re-elect and parties do not make our choices. We do not stay loyal to a party who restricts our rights because they do not approve of our choices. No politician must ever hold us hostage again. We are a country ruled by the majority and our Congress must erase all of their foolish rules that allows any one individual to hold up anything and stop any initiative. No committee should be able to block votes on bills. We need to know how our elected officials are voting on all bills and agreements.

10. How do we, the 99%, really unite? We start by releasing all of our old prejudices. We listen with an open mind to those who offer solutions that are backed up by facts. I listen to Rachel Maddow and Jon Stewart because they quietly discuss the situation with unbelievable facts to back them up. They invite anyone to express their views and are never angry or insulting. Okay, maybe Jon has a few insulting moments but he is backed up by facts (giggles). Next, we must have shared sacrificing because we are all in this economic mix together. There is never a need to hoard because there is more than enough for everyone. Then, we must agree to disagree. Our planet must be protected whether we agree or disagree on global warming. You know the old saying, "Better to be safe than sorry." If we allow the planet to die, we will cease to exist. We need to convert to biofuels which is fuel directly obtained from plants, indirectly from agricultural, domestic, and commercial sources, along with industrial waste. We must wean the planet off of fossil fuels. Those who do not believe in global warming can, at least, agree that we need this planet to live and we must take precautions.

Just because we are the 99%, we must start thinking and place the blame where it truly belongs. Maybe, then we will not keep repeating history. If we do not see the dangers in front of our faces, then we are doomed. If we keep believing the lies and refuse to fact check then we have no hope of redemption. My favorite statement by the Republican hopeful, Governor Mitt Romney, is that yes the economy is recovering but the recovery is too slow.[4] People are suffering too long. Governor Romney has purposely omitted the fact that our recovery is slow because Republican legislators are actively working to kill bills that would allow a speedier recovery. Our recovery is slow because we sit and complain, believe misinformation and react foolishly, and leave unproductive politicians in office forever. All of the 99% treatment is 100% on the 99%. Our unity is our only chance of turning this country in the right direction.

LET'S PRETEND

Let's pretend for just a moment. This is necessary for everyone to get a good laugh at our foolishness. Let's see what life will be like when we make our big decision. We don't have to pretend with Democrats because we already see how life will be. However, if we had rid ourselves of the naysayers and obstructionist, we could have had a really good life. However, it appears the 99% does not want an easier life. So this is our future. If you think the Democratic side is depressing, I am going to present the Republican side and believe me their side will literally kill you, and I mean literally.

So, let's pretend. Republicans have the presidency. Let's make Mitt Romney the President or Newt Gingrich. Okay, I have to tell everyone up front, I will be laughing a lot and sometimes I will laugh so hard I will have to take a nap. So, this section could be rambling. It does not matter which Republican is elected as the president because they all have their marching orders and pledges, of course. So, if you elect one you get them all. Now, along with the Republican President, Congress will be all Republican, just like when Bush II was in office. At least, the 99% will be consistent in their foolishness because they have kept a Republican as President most of the time and our debt has been off the chain but this has been the choice of the 99%. So, we get what we vote for, always.

First, trickle down economy will be the economic blueprint as usual for all previous Republican presidents. We will definitely end up with a huge deficit but, hey, this was our choice. The fact that trickle down has never worked pretty much guarantees that it still will not work again but Republicans are attached to this idea and that is that. (I'm smiling and about to laugh but I have contained myself.) Republicans have never allowed facts to interfere with their ideas. They always go back to their same old failed policies every time they get control, even though our debt goes out of control. They know a large portion of the 99% will never desert them and history has shown that they are correct. For some odd reason, the 99% feels that they are not the target, the other guys are the target. That's how the people of Wisconsin ended up in the fight of their lives.

Therefore, it is necessary for me to be blunt, which I usually am without any urging. WE ARE THE TARGET. Does everyone understand that, yet? (I'm laughing now because I have to keep repeating myself.) History will show that the 99% killed their democracy because they did not have the intelligence to figure out how they were constantly manipulated on every issue. How they kept allowing racism, sexism, homophobia, abortion, and even unions to keep them so divided that they turned the country over to their jailers with their full permission.

Now back to our economic blueprint. Everyone has to remember that the Trickle Down Theory is giving to the wealthy and in their good heart they will share. (Okay, I need a nap right about here because I have been laughing very hard and I am just plain tired. Okay, I'm back and ready to go.) Since we are trickling down, the wealthy will be given more tax breaks and tax havens so they can share, of course. Instead of 83 out of 100 publicly owned corporations paying no taxes,[1] 100 of 100 will pay no taxes. The wealthy tax cuts will be so large that they will pay no taxes either because everyone knows that they share and produce jobs. (Laughing real hard, nap time, I'm back.) Our only revenue will be from the few of the 99% who are working at minimum wage in "Right to work" states. Oh, my bad, I forgot, Republicans will get rid of minimum wage.[2] Anyway, our revenue will be very low, actually it will not exist. That will be okay with big corporations and the 1% because they are global so they do not need the 99% for their profits. (Laughing real hard again, napping, I'm back.) The majority of our jobs will be overseas so that corporations will not have to pay unemployment insurance, healthcare, paid vacations, overtime, sick leave, or pensions. Safety precautions will be eliminated, which are cost effective, and injuries will not be covered. Basically, everything the unions gained for American workers are not necessary with workers in other countries, a win win for the 1%. Either way, jobs will be scarce so the small revenue will be impossible to keep big government operating. Finally, Republicans will get their small government. States will rule (giggles). Since 48 out of 50 states are in debt and with no big government to borrow from, there must be program cuts.

Everyone knows that the first program to be cut will be the Healthcare Bill. However, when this bill is cut, it will be officially named Obamacare so that Republicans can get a real good laugh at their accomplishment. The 99% will be at more free clinics but, like I said, this is okay because the 99% made all of these decisions with their eyes wide open. Those who do not have insurance can still continue to go to hospitals and someone will cover them, though I don't know who that will be. After Obamacare, the Ryan plan will privatize Medicare. Medicare will cost a lot more to senior but that's okay because the 99% is okay with killing grandma. (I was about to laugh until I remembered I'm a grandma. Actually I'm a Nana, but I don't think that name change will save me.) Social Security will be privatized and we will still get our checks but administrative cost will be higher than when the government was the administrator.[3] Instead of getting 99 cents on the dollar, we will be getting around 50 cents on the dollar. That's okay because we made these decisions with our eyes wide open. (I am starting to laugh because I have nothing else to do. Nap time. Okay, I'm back.) All of what I just said is only true if the states can handle Medicare and Social Security. I know Florida can because we have the lottery which is not used for education as promised so there must be enough for old people and young school kids and middle age people. Okay, maybe Florida is not ready. (I am laughing at the seniors of Florida and that has put me into a real beach nap. Okay, I have dusted off the sand and I'm back.)

Actually, all governmental programs have been cut because they have been transferred to the states. Those programs were really eliminated due to lack of funds, but there is just enough for the private companies to be paid their administrative cost. Now, America doesn't look like a good place anymore. As a matter of fact, we finally solved our immigration problem because Mexicans stop coming across the border. No reason since jobs were scarce and the 99% was picking beans now. Also, the few jobs left did not even pay for jumping the fence. Wow! Republican hopeful Governor Mitt Romney was right. Immigrants will self-deport.[4] (I am on the floor laughing and I have collapsed into a self induced nap. Okay, I'm back.) Finally, the 99% might figure out that they made a mistake, but it will not matter because remember, Republicans changed the voting districts and the voting rules. "Just King me now!" I'm kidding, of course, that is what Republicans will be saying. I will not be the King, I will not be the King's court. I will not even be in the Kings courtyard. I will be the peasant. The 99% will be peasants also, White 99% will be a higher peasant than me, but still a peasant. Remember, they already have 'Dead Peasants' insurance on us. It will be like the old plantations with the field Negroes and the house Negroes. (I am howling with laughter because White American thought it would not be them. Okay, I'm back.) We are intertwined, White America, where we go, you go also. Only difference is we see the end of the road, you are still pretending that you have a choice of roads and you don't have any choices left.

When Republicans took over in 2010, every Republican in congress and every Republican governor and their legislature started passing some type of anti-abortion bill. Once they have the presidency, those laws will become the law of the land. (I need a nap because of what is to come for women. Reluctantly, I am back.) They will get rid of all contraceptives, declare a fetus a human, and close Planned Parenthood. Women did not understand that when Republicans talked about smaller government, they were actually talking about the vagina of a women (giggles). So women will be eliminated from most jobs because they will be pregnant all of the time. Obamacare would have been eliminated so pap smears, mammograms, and birth control pills will be costly. Since women will be pregnant all the time, they will have a lot of children, if they survive the pregnancy, of course. There will be little help because Republicans will have done what they always do which is eliminate women and children programs so that the 1% can keep their tax cuts. (I am smiling because this is too sad.) They might even get rid of child support. Who knows? As long as women are the target, Republicans will continue with their mandate.

Okay, even though we have eliminated the social programs and we have women back in the house (giggles), we definitely need an increase to the debt ceiling. With no revenue from most workers in "Right to Work" states and women at home, America is looking scary plus we have no money. The Ryan Budget Plan will be in full force however it will never get us out of debt. Most elderly, who are not the 1%, will be either living on the streets or the back room with their kids. They will be sickly because they will not want to spend their meager Social Security on medicine. (Did I say Social Security? My bad, I was waking from my nap.)

Our infrastructure will look like Europe did after World War II. States can barely afford to keep themselves afloat since most states are in debt now so they will never be able to maintain their infrastructure. Those that live by Nuclear plants might want to relocate immediately. Those by dams need to move today. Railroad tracks should be okay but I wouldn't sleep near any tracks. Any houses close to tracks should move the bedrooms to the opposite side of the trains forward movement. (I have laughed myself into a nap. I'm back.) Let's face it, our environment is about to get real shabby. The entire country is about to become the inner city, a slum, a rundown place, but this was our choice and the Republican mandate.

Okay, I have had enough fun and I'm sure it will never get as bad as I just said but everyone has to admit, it's something to think about. To allow ourselves to be even close to what I just laughed about is scary. It's scary because the 99% does not understand how close we are to what I just described so humorously. The 99% does not have any idea how detrimental losing our majority will be for the fate of this country. Well, only time will tell but here is the good part, for me at least, I do not have that long on this earth to have to endure whatever is in store for the 99%. However, remember and never forget, we are and have always been 100% responsible for our destiny and wherever we are is because we voted to be there. (I am deep into my nap because I have made that "We are responsible" statement too many times.)

Just because we are the 99%, there will be no need for any more of my political books because the 99% either re-elected President Obama or they selected someone else. If President Obama is the man, I sure hope that the 99% surrounds him with representatives who want to work to make the country a better place. If not, then "Let's pretend" is happening and I have no intention of writing about that sad mess. The really sad part about all of this is that this was never about the first Black President. This was always about the 99% because it is always about the 99%. Too bad we pretended and never figured that out.

AFTERWORD

We are the democracy the entire world wants to be. We have the reputation of freedom at its best. However, freedom always breeds laziness. It breeds the assumption that democracy will always be the norm. It allows us to love who we want, work where we want, speak however we want, live however we want, and vote however we want. However, it also makes it more difficult for us to weed out the crazies. This is why we have such a high murder rate and so many criminals. Freedom allows all forms of degeneration into the community and we have all seen examples of that. This is why it is imperative that the 99% remains alert and in charge. Nazi Germany was the classic example of the crazies being in charge. There was no moment of sanity in Nazi Germany yet its good citizens sat and watched until it was too late. This is where we are at this time in history. The 99% must put their subconscious racism aside for just a little while and reject the crazies that are trying to confiscate our society.

Stand still America, WHAP! That was a slap to your face. Wake up, now! Get a grip, please. Pay attention to what is being said to you and at you. This is the moment in history when the 99% can stand up for their integrity. This is the moment when the 99% can stop bullshitting themselves and admit their true feelings. If this is truly a racial issue then admit your racism and move with those who will take you down that path. If, however, you are the 99% who does not want that type of negativity to rule your life then you had better start standing up for this country now. Stop believing the crap about taking the country back because the country you end of with this crazy racists crowd will not be a country you will be able to live in. The solution to our country is as easy as one, two, three. Act like the real 99% and decipher the rhetoric. Register to vote and then actually vote. Select your representative wisely nationally and locally. Since we are 100% responsible for the nation, then lets really be responsible.

Just because we are the 99%, we can make our changes a real "Yes we can" moment. We must elect those who swear they will work with any president so that we can make real changes for the 99%. We must elect those who want the 99% to be strengthen and protected. We must elect those who are trying to help the 99% vote not hinder them with new restrictive rules. We must have what this country is suppose to stand for, equality for all, fairness for all, and respect for all. We must be what we claim we are, the 99%. Just because the President is black is the best time ever to make that claim. We can do it 99%, "YES WE CAN."

ENDNOTES

A Little Something

1. Brady Dennis, Bank of American faces outrage over debit card charge, (http://www. Washingtonpost.com/business/economy/bank-of-america-faces-outrage-over-debit-card-charge/2011/09/03/gIQAp8zGAL story.html)

Year 2011

1. Ann Coulter: 'Our Blacks Are So Much Better Than Their Blacks,' (http://tpmmuckraker.talkingpointsmemo.com/2011/11/ann-coulter-our-blacks-are-so-much-better-than-the.php)
2. Women Voters in the United States, (http://www.america.gov/st/election08-english/2008/April/20080523105153WRybakcuHO.5036737.html)
3. Sulen Miller, Obama Says Republicans Cannot Have the Keys Back to the Car: "No! You Can't Drive." (http://abcnews.go.com/blogs/politics/2010/05/obama-says-republicans-cannot-have-the-keys-back-to-the-car-no-you-cant-drive/)
4. Jake Tapper, Brown: Need to do more; Too Big to Fail, (http://blogs.abcnews.com/politicalpunch/2010/04/brown-need-to-do-more-on-too-big-to-fail.html)
5. Brianna Golodruga, America's Banks: Doomed to Fail?, (http://abcnews.go.com/Business/story?id=70371368page=1)
6. Jeff Mason, Obama says he inherited economic problems, (http://www.reuters.com/article/2011/08/09/us-crisis-obama-debt-idUSTRE7776D620110809)
7. Matthew Jaffe, R.I.P., TARP: Government Rescue Ends Sunday, (http://abcnews.go.com/Poltiics/tarp-government-bailout-ends-sunday-started-bush-gop/story?id=11765955)

8. Greg Sargent, Obama hits McConnell "one-term president" claim, (http://voices.washingtonpost.com/plum-line/2010/10/obama_nits_mcconnell_one_term.html)

9. Douglas V. Gibbs, GOP Candidates in Iowa: No New Taxes, (http://politicalpistachio.blogspot.com/2011/08/gop-candidate-iowa-no-new-taxes.html)

10. Robert Sobel, Fox News host calls Occupy Wall Street movement "Domestic terrorists," (http://www/examiner.com/liberal-in-orlando/fox-news-host-calls-occupy-wall-street-movement-domestic-terrorists)

11. Ben Craw, MSNBC and Fox Apparently of Different Minds On Occupy Wall Street, (http://www.huffingtonpost.com/2011/11/18/msnbc-and-fox-of-different-minds-on-occupy-wall-street_n_1100741.html)

12. Robert Farley, Republicans Philosophy of Deregulation to Blame for Runaway Greed, Crash, Bailouts, (http://voices.yahoo.com/republicans-philosophy-deregulation-blame-for-2035584.html)

13. William Briggs, With Republicans in office. Downhill slide will continue, (http://www.mauinews.com/page/content.detail/id/551921)

14. Liz Halloran and Frank James, White House Threatens Veto of "Cut, Cap, Balance' Bill; GOP Plows ahead, (http://www.npr.org/blogs/it sallpolitics/2011/07/19/138486765/white-house-threatens-veto-on-cap-cut-balance-bill)

It's on Us Buddy

1. Sulen Miller, Obama Says Republicans Cannot Have the Keys Back to the Car: "No! You Can't Drive." (http://abcnews.go.com/blogs/politics/2010/05/obama-says-republicans-cannot-have-the-keys-back-to-the-car-no-you-cant-drive/)

2. The Clinton Presidency: Historic Economic Growth, (http://clinton5.nara.gov/WH/Acomplishment/eightyears-03.html)

3. Kelly Wallace, President Clinton announces another record surplus; CNN White House, (http://articles.cnn.com/2000-09_27/clinton.surplus_1_budget-surplus-national-debt-fiscal-discipline?_s=pm:allpolitics)

4. Increases in National Debt, (http://www.lafn.org/gvdc/Natl_Debt_Chart.html)

5. Reaganomics, (http://www.investorwords.com/4052/reaganomics. html)
6. POLITICS:Bush II Administration's unpaid for policies will continue to add trillions to our deficit, (http://conservativereport. com/2010/01/ 15/politics-bush-ii-administration-%E2%80%Cunpaid-for-policies-will-continue-to-add-trillions-to our deficit%E2%80%9D/)
7. Zaid Jilani, Top Reagan Economic Advisor: Return to Clinton-Era Tax Rates Would Not Hurt Economic Growth, (http://thinkprogress.org/ economy/2011/06/02/234238/conservative-myth-taxes-growth/)
8. Brian Montopoli, Ronald Reagan Myth Doesn't Square with Reality, (http://www.cbsnews.com/8301_503544_162_20030729-503544. html/)
9. Racism and the Republican Party, (http://www.anotherperspective. org/advoc268.html)
10. Faiz Shakir, Limbaugh: 'I Hope Obama Fails,' (http://thinkprogress. org/politics/2009/01/20/35012/limbaugh-obama-fails/)
11. Recall of State Officials, (http://www.ncsl.org/default.aspx?tabid -16581)

It's the Economy, Stupid

1. Kelly Wallace, $1.35 trillion tax cut becomes laws, (http://articles. cnn.com/2001-06-07/politics/bush.taxes_1_child-tax-credit-trillion-tax-cut-relief?_s=PM:ALLPOLITICS)
2. Paul Krugman, Bush tax cut mythology, (http://Krugman.blogs. nytimes.com/2008/01/14/bush-tax-cuts-mythology/)
3. Republicans: Unemployment Benefits Must be Paid For, But Tax Cuts for the Rich Don't, (http://chattahbox.com/us/2010/07/14/republicans-unemployment-must-be-paid-for-but-tax-cuts-for-the-rich-don't/)
4. Joel Friedman & Isaac Shapiro, Tax Returns: A Comprehensive Assessment of the Bush Administration's Record on Cutting Taxes, (http://www.cbpp.org/cms/index.cfm?fa=view&id=1811)
5. President Barack Obama says Rep. Paul Ryan voted for wars, tax cuts and a drug bill that weren't paid for, (http://www.politifact.com/ wisconsin/statements/2011/apr/27/barack-obama/President-barack-obama-says-rep-paul-ryan-voted-wa/)

6. Alex Seitz-Ward, Obama Created More Jobs in One Year Than Bush Created in Eight, (http://thinkprogress.org/politics/2011/01/07/137866/obama-more-jobs-bush)

7. Dennis Jacobe, Energy States Lead in Job Creation, Financial States Struggle, (http://www.gallup.com/poll/149072/energy-states-lead-job-creation-financial-states-struggle-aspx)

8. Kent Klein, Obama: End Tax Breaks For Companies Sending Jobs Overseas, (http://www.voanews.com/english/news/Obama-Says-Tax-Code-Changes-Promote-Jobs-in-US—105096329.html)

9. Joan McCarter, How GOP votes unanimously to protect big oil subsidies, (http://www.dailykos.com/story/2011/03/01/951571/-House-GOP-votes-unanimously-to-protect-big-oil-subsidies)

10. Tax Data, February 10, 2009, State debt per capita as percent of state's GDP, (http://www.taxfoundation.org/taxdata/show/268.html)

11. Cassandra Vinograd, News of the World: UK Policies Put Phone Hacking Victims At Around 800, (http://www.huffingtonpost.com/2011/12/10/news-of-the-world-uk-poli_n_1140770.html)

12. Pat Garofalo, Disregarding Their Promise To Focus On Jobs, Republicans Aim To Abolish Job Training Programs, (http://thinkprogress.org/economy/2011/01/25/173749/gop-job-training/)

13. U.S. National Unemployment by Political Party/President, (http://www.truthfulpolitics.com/comments/u-s-national-unemployment-by-political-party-president/)

14. Republicans refuse to work toward solutions, (http://www.bonnercountydailybee.com/opinion/letters_to_editor/article_8ff52abe-0b67-11e1-8ac9=001cc4c002e0.html)

15. Republicans Consistently Vote Against Own Policies, (http://www.americaforpurchase.com/republicans/republicans-consistently-vote-against-own-policies/)

16. State Balanced Budget Requirement; National Conference of State Legislators,(http://www.ncsl.org/default.aspx?tabid=12660)

17. Julia Edwards, Thanks, but No Thanks: Why Some States Are Refusing Federal Money, (http://www.nationaljournal.com/thanks-but-no-thanks-why-some-states-are-refusing-federal-money-20110310)

18. Domenick Pilla, Republicans block unemployment benefits extension for lazy drug addicted breeding hobos-VIDEO, (http://www.examiner.com/cultural-issues-in-national/republicans-block-unemployment-benefits-extension-for-lazy-drug-addicted-breeding-hobos-video)

19. The Republicans Promised Jobs During The Midterms, (http://www.dailykos.com/story/2010/11/04/917515/-The-Republican-Promised-Jobs-During-The-Midterms)

20. GOP's First Five Months: No Jobs Bills, (http://democraticleader.gov/news/reports?id=0526

21. Mr. Congressman, where are the jobs?, (http://www.examiner.com/economic-policy-in-national/mr-congressman-where-are-the-jobs)

Jobs, What Jobs

1. United States GDP Growth Rate, (http://www.tradingeconomics.com/united-states-gdp-growth)

2. The Republicans Promised Jobs During The Midterms, (http://www.dailykos.com/story/2010/11/04/917515/-The-Republicans-Promised-Jobs-During-The-Miterm)

3. Robert Bowen, Mr. Congressman, where are the jobs?, (http://www.examiner.com/economic-policy-in-national/mr-congressman-where-are-the-jobs)

4. GOP's First Five Months: No Jobs Bills, (http://www.democraticleader.gov/news/reports?id=0526

5. Richest Tenth own 85% of World's Asset, In Terms of Wealth, US Most Unequal, (http://www.timesoline.co.uk/tol/news/world/asia/article661055.ece)

6. Day 118: House Republicans Priority Still Isn't Job Creation, (http://www.dccc.org/blog/entry/day_118_house_republican_priority_still_isnt_job_creation/)

7. GOP's First Five Months: No Jobs Bills, (http://www.democraticleader.gov/news/reports?id=0526

8. Andrew Taylor, Republicans kill Senate jobless aid measure, (http://www.msnbc.msn.com/id/37904586/ns/politics-capitol_hill/t/republicans-kill-senate-jobless-aid-measure/)

9. GOP's First Five Months: No Jobs Bills, (http://www.democraticleader.gov/news/reports?id=0526

10. Randy Cohen, Too Much Vacation for Congress?, (http://ethicist.blogs.nytimes.com/2009/08/03/too-much-vacation-for-congress/)

11. Michael Cohn, Obama Sends Jobs Bill with Tax Cuts to Congress, (http://www.acountingtoday.com/news/obama-sends-jobs-bill-with-tax-cuts-to-congress-59953-1.html)
12. Paul Wiseman, Localities still shedding jobs, (http://dailyreporter.com/2011/06/06/localities-still-shedding-jobs/)
13. Employment Situation Summary, (http://www.bls.gov/news.release/emsit.nr0.htm)
14. David Dwyer, Double Standard? Romney, Perry Grew State Payrolls as Governor, (http://abcnews.go.com/blogs/politics/2011/09/double-standard-romney-perry-grew-state-payrolls-as-governor?)
15. Brian Beutler, Republicans Governors Quietly Accept Federal Dollars-While Attacking Federal Spending,(http://tpmdc.talkingpointsmemo.com/2011/04/republicans-governors-quietly-accept-federal-dollars-despite-spending-attacks.php)
16. Pat Garofalo, Gov Rick Scott Says He May Reject Federal Funding He Already Applied For, (http://thinkprogress.org/educator/2011/10/24/352039/rick scott-race-to-the-top-reject-again/)
17. Gary Langer, Obama gains vs GOP on Jobs as Congress Hits a New Low, (http://abcnews.go.com/blogs/politics/2011/10/obama-gains-vs-gop-on-jobs-as-congress-hits-a-new-low)
18. Lloyd Dunkelberger, State may consider changes to public employee heath benefits to save money, (http://htpolitics.com/2011/10/21/state-may-consider-changes-to-public-employee-health-benefits-to-save-money/)
19. Supreme Court Decision in Wal-Mart Class-Action Claim Brings Praise, Anger, (http://www.foxnews.com/politics/2011/06/20/groups-blast-laud-high-court-for-decision-against-nations-largest/)
20. Jeff Gelles, Bank Transfer Day a boom to credit unions, small banks, (http://www.philly.com/philly/news/133311428.html)
21. Where You Can Buy Made In America Building Products, (http://abcnews.go.com/blogs/business/2011/10/how-to-build-a-made-in-america-home)
22. Rev. Edward Pinkney, Whirlpool slashed jobs; Boycott Whirlpool, (http://www.peoplestribune.org/PT.2006.06/PT.2006.06.17.html)

Legislators from Hell

1. S.J. Gulitti, Scott Walker, Conservative Hero Propped Up By the Kock Brothers, (http://my.firedoglake.com/sjgulitti/2011/02/223/scott-walker-conservative-hero-propped-up-by-the-Kock-brothers/)
2. James Kelleher, NEWSMAKER-Wisconsin governor's policies polarize state, (http://www.reuters.com/article/2011/03/10/wisconsin-walker-idUSN0929450020110310)
3. Joel Wendland, 100 Days: Wisc. Gov. Scott Walker's Job-killing Record, (http://www.politicalaffairs.net/100-days-wisc-gov-scott-walker-s-job-killing-record/)
4. Peter Fenn, Tea Party Funding Kock Brothers Emerge From Anonymity, (http://www.usnews.com/opinion/blogs/Peter-Fenn/2011/02/02/tea-party-funding-kock-brothers-emerge-from-anonymity)
5. The Lavish Life of Teachers, (http://a-teachers-view.blogspot.com/2011/03/lavish-ilfe-of-teachers.html)
6. Joel Wendland, 100 Days: Wisc. Gov. Scott Walker's Job-killing Record, (http://www.politicalaffairs.net/100-days-wisc-gov-scott-walker-s-job-killing-record/)
7. Kevin Dolak, Wisconsin Recall: GOP Retains Senate Control, (http://abcnews.go.com/Politics/wisconsin-recall-gop-retain-senate-control/story?id=14269209)
8. Outsiders spend millions on Wisconsin recall elections, (http://news.yahoo.com/outsiders-spend-millions-on-wisconsin-recall-elections-042423764.html)
9. Patricia Hensley, Fire Michigan Governor Rick Synder recall campaign update, (http://www.examiner.com/political-buzz-in-ann-arbor/fire-michigan-governor-rick-snyder-campaign-update)
10. Robin Marty, Michigan Governor Starts "Financial Marshal Law" is Wisconsin Next?, (http://www.care2.com/causes/politics/blog/michigan-governor-starts-financial/)
11. Jane Akre, Medicare Fraud's Rick Scott leading in Florida Gov. Race, (http://news.injuryboard.com/medicare-fraud-rick-scott-leading-in-florida-gov-race-aspx?goggled=282152)
12. Stacey Singer, Gov. Rick Scott's drug testing policy stirs suspicion, (http://www.palmbeachpost.com/money/gov-rick-scott-drug-testing-policy-stirs-suspicion-1350922.html)

13. Lizete Alvarez, Miami-Dade County Mayor is Removed, (http://www.nytimes.com/2011/03/16/us/16miami.html)

14. Chris Christie Announces Plan to Privatize New Jersey Schools, (http://www.huffingtonpost.com/2011/06/11/chris-christie-schools_n_875262.html)

15. Sven Larson, Federal Funds and State Fiscal Independence, (http://www.heritage.org/research/reports/2008/05/federal-funds-and-state-fiscal-independence)

16. Peter Rothstein, Guest Post: Politics Obscures Policy in New Jersey RGGI Battle, (http://www.greentechmedia.com/articles/read/guest-post-politics-obscures-policy-in-new-jersey-rggi-battle/)

17. Doug Mataconis, Georgia's New Immigration Law Leading To Crops Rotting in Farmers Fields, (http://www.outsidethebeltway.com/georgias-new-immigration-law-leading-tocrops-rotting-in-farmers-fields/)

18. Alabama to enforce strict immigration laws, (http://www'cbsnews.com/stories/2011/09/29/earlyshow/main20113223.shtml/)

19. Mississippi Personhood Law Proposes To Make Abortion, Birth Control, IVF Illegal (http://gothamist.com/2011/10.26/latest_threat_to_women_rights_to_ch.php)

20. Ohio Gov. Kasich Apologizes to Police Officer He Called 'Idiot', (http://www.politicsdaily.com/2011/02/17/ohio-gov-kasich-apologizes-to-police-officer-he-called-id/)

21. Jeff Simon, Kasich unloads on LeBron, Declares Mavericks 'honorary Ohioans,' (http://politicalticker.blogs.cnn.com/2011/06/13/kasich-unloads-on-lebron-declares-mavericks-honorary-ohioans/)

22. Gov. Kasich fights for S.B.5 at Tony Packo's, (http://www.northwestohio.com/news/story.aspx?id=668832)

23. Glenn Thrush, Ohio Senate Bill 5's repeal buoys Democrats, (http://www.politico.com/news/stories/1111/67918.html)

24. David Badaesh, Mitch Daniels—Supposed Moderate—Announces He Will Not Run, (http://thenewcivilrightsmovement.com/mitch-daniels-supposed-moderate-announces-he-will-not-run/politics/2011/05/22/20655)

25. Katherine Hunter, GOP governors trim state employees' bargaining clout, (http://www.stateline.org/live/ViewPage.action?siteNodeId=136&languageId=1&contentId=15997)

26. Are Republicans Manipulating Redistricting Software To Thwart Voters Will, (http://www.beachpeanuts.com/2011/07/florida-gop-manipulating-redistricting-software-to-thwart-voters-will)
27. The Confederate Flag: Symbol of Culture or Racism, (http://ecarson.wordpress.com/2007/12/05/the-confederate-flag-symbol-of-culture-or-racism)
28. GOP's First Five Months: No New Jobs, (http://www.democraticleader.gov/news/reports?id=0526
29. Sean Collins, G.O.P. Bid to Void Light Bulb Law Fails, (http://www.nytimes.com/2011/07/13/business/energy-environment/republicans-fail-to-annul-new-light-bulb-law)
30. Day 118: House Republicans Priority Still Isn't Job Creation, (http://www.dccc.org/blog/entry/day_118_house_republican_priority_still_isnt_job_creation/)
31. Jim Worth, "Are Republican Governor's Killing American," (http://02d30f6.netsolhost.com/blog1/?p=3077)
32. For Obama, a Record on Diversity but Delays on Judicial Confirmations: rss broadcast, (http://rssbroadcast.com/?p=59636
33. 2010 Minnesota Governor's Race, (http://politicsinminnesota.com/2010-mn-governor-race/)
34. Dayton Signs Bill Ending MN Gov't Shutdown, (http://www.northlandsnewscenter.com/news/local/Shutdown-Ends-With-125890423.html)

Way To Go, 99%

1. Lauren V. Burke, I.D. Required, (http://politic365.com/2011/06/05/republican-governor-change-voting-laws-in-prep-for-2012/)
2. Ed Morrissey, Senate Republicans promise filibusters until tax issue resolved, (http://hotair.com/archives/2010/12/01/senate-republicans-promise-filibuster-until-tax-issue-resolved/)
3. President Obama: Tax Cuts for Wealthy are Republicans' 'Holy Grail,' (http://abcnews.go.com/Politics/tax-cuts-deal-pits-president-obama-democrats/story?id=12332116)
4. Steve Benen, Senate GOP protects oil industry subsidies, (http://www.washingtonmonthly.com/political-animal/2011_5/senate_gop_protects_oil_indust029647.php)

5. Big Oil's $38 billion defense, (http://money.cnn.com/2011/04/29/news/companies/big-oil-gas-price-response/index.htm)

6. Donald Carr, Farm subsidies paid to the members of the 112th Congress, (http://huffingtonpost.com/donald-carr/farm-subsidies-paid-to-112-congress_b_842704.html)

7. On the debt-ceiling deal, (http://economist.com/blogs/democracyinamerica/2011/08/deficit-reduction)

8. Republicans Consistently Vote Against Own Policies, (http://www.americaforpurchase.com/republicans/republicans-consistently-vote-against-own-policies/)

9. Algernon Austin, Paul Ryan's Budget Plan: Trillions for the Rich, Pain for Everyone Else, (http://www.huffingtonpost.com/algernon-austin/paul-ryans-budget-plan-tr_b_847984.html)

10. Lisa Mascaro and Christi Parsons, GOP holds reins in debate over tax cuts extension, (http://articles.latimes.com/2010/dec/01/nation/la-na-tax-cuts-20101202)

11. Dems, GOP threaten government shutdown, (http://www.thehour.com/story/499648)

12. Eliza, Why Raising the Debt Ceiling Might Not Be Enough, (http://abcnews.go.com/blogs/2011/07/why-raising-the-debt-ceiling-might-not-be-enough/)

13. Jonathan Karl, John Parkinson and Huma Khan, House Republicans Cave on Payroll Tax Cut Extension, (http://abcnews.go.com/Politics/house-republicans-cave-on-payroll-tax-cuts-extension-obama/story?id=15212988)

14. Michael Cohn, Obama Sends Jobs Bill with Tax Cuts to Congress, (http://www.acountingtoday.com/news/obama-sends-jobs-bill-with-tax-cuts-to-congress-59953-1.html)

15. Republicans: Unemployment Benefits Must be Paid For, But Tax Cuts for the Rich Don't, (http://chattahbox.com/us/2010/07/14/republicans-unemployment-must-be-paid-for-but-tax-cuts-for-the-rich-don't/)

I Sure Hope You're Satisfied

1. Rick Perry says Barack Obama is a socialist, (http://www.politifact.com/truth-o-meter/statement/2012/jan/08/rick-perry-says-barack-obama-socialists/)

2. Barack Obama's US Senate Facts, Not the Hype, (http://most liberalsenator.blogspot.com?)

3. Michael Tomasky, The Meltdown's True Villain, (http://www.the dailybeast.com/articles/2011/08/05/economics-meltdown-villain-george-w-bush-s-staggering-debt-numbers.html)

4. POLITICS:Bush II Administration's unpaid for policies will continue to add trillions to our deficit, (http://conservativereport.com/2010/01/15/politics-bush-ii-administration-%E2%80%Cunpaid-for-policies-will-continue-to-add-trillions-to our deficit%E2%80%9D/)

5. Andrew Leonard, Don't believe the Obama big spending hype,(http://politics.salon.com/2011/04/27/the_big_obama_spending_lie/)

6. Julianna Goldman and Hans Nichols, Obama Outlaws Regulations Overhaul to Sabe Business About $10 Billion, (http://www.bloomberg.com/news/2011-01-23/obama-to-outline-regulatory-overhaul-details-to-save-10-billion.html)

7. Obama created more jobs in one year than Bush created in eight, (http://thinkprogress.org/romm/2011/01/08/207311/obama-created-more-jobs-in-one-year-than-bush-created-in-eight)

8. Health Statistics Death form cancer (most recent) by country, (http://www.nationmaster.com/graph/hea_dea_fro_can_health-death-from-cancer)

9. Ohio Gov Kasich let wild animal regulations lapse, (http://www.dailykos.com;story/2011/10/19/1028141/-ohio-Gov-Kasich-let-wild-animal-regulations-lapse)

10. Lisa Lerer, Congress Prepares Bill to Remove Oil-Spill Liability Limit—Bloomberg, (http://www.bloomberg.com/news/2010-06-03/democrats-prepare-bill-to-remove-75million-damages-limit-for-oil-spills.html)

11. Obama BP Meeting: Company agrees to 20 billion Escrow Account for Victims, (http://www.huffingtonpost.com/2010/06/16/obama-bp-meeting-presiden_n_613856.htm)l

12. Coal-Ash Disasters Spur Rules Showdown, (http://www.bloomberg.com/news/2011-11-03/coal-ash-disasters-spur-rules-showdown.html)

13. Gaius Publius, Hedge fund king John Paulson earns more per hour than most Americans in a lifetime-and he pays a lower tax rare, (http://www.americanblog.com/2011/05/hedge-fund-king-john-paulson-earns-more.html)

14. Hrafnkell Haraldson, 1 Day Tax Cuts for Millionaires Equals Feeding Needy for 1 Year, (http://www.politicususa.com/en/tax-cuts-millionaires-feeding-needy)

15. Andy Bromeje, Sanders Proposes Legislation to Make Rich Pay more Into Social Security, (http:/7dblogs.com/blurt/2011/08/Sanders-proposes-legislation-to-make-wealthy-pay-more-social-security.html)

16. Most American Say U.S. Headed in Wrong Direction, (http://blogs.wsj.com/economics/2010/01/14/most-americans-say-U-S-headed-in-wrong-direction/)

17. Matthew Jaffe, R.I.P., TARP: Government Rescue Ends Sunday, (http://abcnews.go.com/Poltiics/tarp-government-bailout-ends-sunday-started-bush-gop/story?id=11765955)

18. POLITICS:Bush II Administration's unpaid for policies will continue to add trillions to our deficit, (http://conservativereport.com/2010/01/15/politics-bush-ii-administration-%E2%80%Cunpaid-for-policies-will-continue-to-add-trillions-to our deficit%E2%80%9D/)

19. Brian Beutler, Republicans Governors Quietly Accept Federal Dollars-While Attacking Federal Spending, (http://tpmdc.talking pointsmemo.com/2011/04/republicans-governors-quietly-accept-federal-dollars-despite-spending-attacks.php)

20. Israel should heed Obama plan, (http://articles.boston.com/2011-05-23/bostonglobe/29574922_1_president_obama-palestinian-state-final-status-negotiations)

21. Presidential vacations: How does Obama compare?, (http://www.cbsnews.com/stories/2011/08/17/eveningnews/main20093801.html)

22. Rachel Weiner, The Ten Most Egregious FOX News Distortions (VIDEO), (http://www.huffingtonpost.com/2009/10/20/the-ten-most-egregious-fo_n_321740.htm?)

23. FOX Calls Obama's Fist Bump a "Terrorist Fist Bump," (http://www.youtube.com/Watch?v=TpdlfzEN_JO)

24. It is the Middle Class, Stupid, (http://catsnjammer64.wordpress.com/2012/01/13/it-is-the-middle-class-stupid/)

25. Naureen Khan, Sarah Huisenga, NAACP leader blasts Gingrich's food stamp comment, (http://www.cbsnews.com/8301-503544-5734055-503544/naacp-leader-blasts-gingrichs-food-stamp-comment/)

26. Psycho Talk: FOX's David Asman Accuses Young Obama of Gaming the System on College Scholarships, (http://www.youtube.com/watch?v=jyfvbiiQ_Vc)

27. Jon Stewart debated Bill O'Reilly about Common: Behold, the trumped-up outrage, (http://watching.tv.ew.com/2011/05/16/jon-stewart-bill-oreilly-common/)
28. Rush Limbaugh: Liberals Wouldn't Care If Casey Anthony's Child Had Died In The Womb, (http://www.huffingtonpost.com/2011/07/07/rush-limbaugh-wo_n_892207.htm)
29. Right-Wingers Rush to Label Arizona Shooting Suspect a Liberal-While Simultaneously Accusing Left of "Politicizing" Assassination Attempt, (http://firedoglake.com/2011/01/09/right-wingers-rush-to-label-arizona-shooting-suspect-a-liberal-while-simultaneously-accusing-left-of-politicizing-assassination-attempt/)
30. Ali Gharib and Travis Waldron, Right-Wing Pundits Jumped To Blame Muslims And "Jihadists" For Norway Attack, (http://thinkprogress.org/security/2011/07/23/277310/wapos-jen-rubin-wsj-right-wing-pundits-jumped-to-blame-muslims-and-jihadists-for-norway-attack/)

State of the Union

1. Lawrence Mishel and Matthew Walters, How unions help all workers, (http://www.epi.org/publications/entry/briefingpapers_bp143/)
2. Gordon Lafer, What 'Right to Work' means to Indiana Workers: A Paycut, (http://www.thenation.com/article/165599/what-right-work-means-indiana-workers-pay-cut)
3. Heather, Are 'Dead Peasant' Life Insurance Policies Fair?, (http://videocafe.crooksandliars.com/heather/abc-news-are-dead((-peasant-life-insurance-poli)

You Can Trust Me

1. Jon Ward, Big Government Gets Bigger, (http://www.washingtontimes.com/news/2008/oct/19/big-government-gets-bigger/)
2. Jim Worth, "Are Republican Governor's Killing American," (http://02d30f6.netsolhost.com/blog1/?p=3077)
3. Matt Hadro, CNN's Cafferty: Are Republicans Debate Crowds Bloodthirsty?, ea (http://www.mrc.org/biasalert/2011/20110927075902.aspx)

Oops, Wrong Turn

1. Mackenzie Weinger, Poll: 73 percent of Americans say country headed in wrong direction, (http://www.politics.com/news/stories/0811/61031.html)

It's A Deal

1. Agence France-Presse, Highlights of New U.S. Trade Deals to China, (http://www.industryweek.com/articles/highlights_of_new_u-s-trade_deals_to_china_23683.aspx)

Pay Up or Else

1. Armand Biroonak, 2000-20008 Job Growth Slowest Since The Depression, (http://www.ourfuture.org/fast-fact/2008104427/2000-2008-job-growth-slowest-depression)
2. Day 118: House Republicans Priority Still Isn't Job Creation, (http://www.dccc.org/blog/entry/day_118_house_republicans_priority_still_isnt_job_creation/)
3. Rosalind S. Helderman & David Nakamura, Obama's jobs bill stalled in Senate, (http://washingtonpost.com/politics/obama-jobs-bill-stalled-in-senate/2011/10/11/gIQAIoJmdL_story.html?hpid=z38wpisre=nl_wonk)
4. Algernon Austin, Paul Ryan's Budget Plan: Trillions for the Rich, Pain for Everyone Else, (http://www.huffingtonpost.com/algernon-austin/paul-ryans-budget-plan-tr_b_847984.html)
5. S&P Downgrades U.S. Debt Rating-Press Release, (http://blogs.wsj.com/marketbeat/2011/08/05/sp-downgrades-u-s-debt-rating-press-release/)
6. S&P Downgrades U.S. Debt Rating-Press Release, (http://blogs.wsj.com/marketbeat/2011/08/05/sp-downgrades-u-s-debt-rating-press-release/)
7. Super Committee Automatic Spending Cuts Triggers May Be Blocked By Congress, (http://www.huffingtonpost.com/2011/11/21/super-committee-deadline-automatic-cuts-trigger_n_1104994.html)

8. Leo Kapakos, The Super committee failure is a win for President Obama, (http://www.examiner.com/political-buzz-in-new-york/a-failure-for-the-super-committee-is-a-win-for-president-obama)

9. Laura Clawson, Republicans leaving FAA shutdown and thousands out of work through August, (http://www.dailykos.com/story/2011/08/02/1002184/-Republicans-leaving-FAA-shutdown-and-thousands-out-of-work-through-august)

10. Brian Merchant, The GOP Anti-Clean Air Act Bill is an Assault on Science Itself, (http://www.treehugger.com/corporate-responsibility/the-gop-anti-clean-air-act-bill-is-an-assault-on-science-itself.html)

11. Michael Cohn, Obama Sends Jobs Bill with Tax Cuts to Congress, (http://www.acountingtoday.com/news/obama-sends-jobs-bill-with-tax-cuts-to-congress-59953-1.html)

12. Tamara Keith, Congress May Back Bill On It's Own Insider Trading, (http://www.npr.org/2012/02/01/146239874/bill-banning-congressional-insider-trading-has-bipartisanship-support)

It's a Private Matter

1. ABOUT THE FCAT, (http://fcat.fldoe.org/aboutfcat/english/about3.html)

2. Stephanie Mencimer, Rick Scott's School Plan for Scoundrels, (http://motherjones.com/politics/2010/12/rick-scott-florida-education-jeb-bush)

3. Nicholas Johnson, Phil Oliff and Erica Williams, An Update on State Budget Cuts, (http://www.cbpp.org/cms/index.cfm?fa=view&id=1214)

4. Liam Dillon, Cities Pay for Stadiums Abandoned by Teams, (http://www.voiceofsandiego.org/government/thehall/article_03b1a146-bb7b-11df-877d-001cc4c002e0.html)

5. Charlie Cain & Gary Heinlein, Bulging prisons drain Michigan's budget, (http://www.capps-mi.org/clips/material%20to%20put%20up/Bulging%20prisons%20drain.htm)

6. Who Profits from the Prison Boom?, (http://www.miroundtable.org/National%20Articles/Who%20Profits%20from,htm)

7. Rania Khalek, The Shocking Ways the Corporate Prison Industry Games the System, (http://www.alternet.org/rights/153212/the

shocking ways the corporate prison industry games the system?
page=2)

8. The perverse incentives of private prisons, (http://www.economist.
com/blogs/democracyinamerica/2010/08/private_prisons)

9. Steven Hawkins, Education vs Incarceration, (http://prospect.org/
article/education-vs-incarceration)

10. James Roosevelt Jr., Social Security's Enduring Truths, (http://www.
aarp.org/bulletin/2011/06/)

11. Zaid Jilani, A Manufactured 'Crisis:' Congress Can Let The Post
Office Save Itself Without Mass Layoffs Or Service Reductions,
(http://thinkprogress.org/economy/2011/09/28/330524/postal-non-
crisis-post-office-save-itself/)

12. Privatizing the US Postal Service, (http://www.progress.org/2011/
fedex.htm)

13. Ezra Klein, Study: Privatizing government doesn't actually save money,
(http://www.washingtonpost.com/blogs/ezra-klein/post/study-
privatizing-government-doesnt-actually-save-money/2011/09/15/
gIQA2rpZUK_blog.html)

14. House Republicans Torn Over Paying For Storm Aid Package, (http://
www.huffingtonpost.com/2011/05/26/missouri-tornado-storm-aid-
republicans-divided_n_867613.htm)

15. Jon Bershad, Gov. Christie Slams Congress Over FEMA Budget
Debate: 'People Are Suffering Now,' (http://www.mediaite.com/
gov-christie-slams-congress-over-fema-budget-debate-people-are-
suffering-now/)

16. GEO Exective Calabrese selling millions of dollars in property, (http://
www.texasprisonbidness.org/blogging-categories/money?page=8)

17. Mark Kroll, CEO Pay Rates, (http://www.cab.latech.edu/-mkroll/
510-papers/fall-05/Group6.pdf)

Foreign Affairs

1. Christopher Alexander, Tunisia's protest wave: where it comes from and
what it means, (http://mideast.foreignpolicy.com/posts/2011/01/02/
tunisia_s_protest_wave_where_it_comes_from_and_what_it_
means_for_ben_ali)

2. Ken Dilanian, Boehner credits Obama for handling of Egypt crisis, (http://articles.latimes.com/2011/feb/14/world/la-fg-obama-egypt-20110214)
3. Thousands in Yemen Protest Against the Government, (http://www.nytimes.com/2011/01/28/world/middleeast/28yemen.html
4. Obama 'could not ignore' Libya crisis, (http://www.iol.co.za/news/africa/obama-could-not-ignore-libya-crisis-1.1048595)
5. David Neiwert, Fox & Friends want to be sure everyone gives George W. Bush credit for Bin Laden's death, (http://crooksandliars.com/davd-neiwert/fox-friends-giving-george-w-bush-credit-for-bin-ladens-death)
6. Bush Not Concerned About Bin Laden, (http://www.politicolnews.com/bush-not-concerned-about-bin-laden/)
7. Israel should heed Obama plan, (http://articles.boston.com/2011-05-23/bostonglobe/29574922_1_president_obama_palestinian)

Give it a Rest

1. Carrie Underwood On Why She'll Never Tweet and Her Connection To Reese Witherspoon, (http://www.accesshollywood.com/Carrie-underwood-on-why-shell-never-tweet-and-her-connection-to-reese-witherspoon_article_24551
2. Welcome to the Dream Act Portal, (http://dreamact.info)
3. Tanya Somanader, Romney: Any Concern For Income Inequality Is 'About Envy,' (http://thinkprogress.org/economy/2012/01/11/402671/romney-any-concern-for-income-inequality-is-about-envy/)
4. King James Version, Mark 10:25
5. Kevin G. Hall, Foreclosure Help: Are Most Wall Street Tycoons Criminally Liable, (http://udolegal.com/udolegal.news/feature-headlines/foreclosure-help-are-more-wall-street-tycoons-criminally-liable.html)
6. Starbucks CEO Howard Schultz Calls For Boycott On Campaign Contributions, (http://www.huffingtonpost.com/2011/08/15/starbucks-howard-schultz-boycott-campaign-contributions_n_927550.html)

The Pledge

1. Ari Shapiro, The Man Behind the GOP's No-Tax Pledge, (http://www.npr.org/2011/07/14/13780071/the-man-behind-the-gop-tax-pledge)
2. Stacy Curtain, Corporate America Pays a Lot Less in Taxes Than You Think, (http://finance.yahoo.com/blogs/daily-ticker/corporate-america-pays-lot-less-taxes-think-125020207.html)
3. Hrafnkell Haraldsson, 1 Day Tax Cuts for Millionaires Equals Feeding Needy for 1 Year, (http://www.politicususa.com/en/tax-cuts-millionaires-feeding-needy)
4. Julie Rovner, GOP Hopefuls Divided Over Anti-Abortion Pledge, (http:www.npr.org/2011/06/23/137350265/gop-hopefuls-divided-over-anti-abortion-pledge)
5. Alison Harding, Santorium Signs Pro-Marriage Pledge Promising Personal Fidelity, (http://www.kcci.com/r/28497335/detail.html)
6. The Pledge, (http://www.cutcapbalanceact.com/)
7. John Whitesides, Republicans pledge allegiance—often, (http://www.reuters.com/articles/2011/07/13/us-usa-campaign-pledges-idUSTRE76C67E20110713)
8. Laura Bassett, Newt Gingrich signs Fetal Personhood Pledge, (http://www.huffingtonpost.com/2011/12/14/newt-gingrich-personhood-pledge_n_1149615.html)

Think of Something

1. Melissa Boteach and Seth Hanlon, Congress Chooses One Weeks's Worth of Tax Cuts for Millionaires over Nutrition Assistance, (http://www.americanprogress.org/issues/2011/06/bait_and_switch.html)
2. Hrafnkell Haraldsson, 1 Day Tax Cuts for Millionaires Equals Feeding Needy for 1 Year, (http://www.politicususa.com/en/tax-cuts-millionaires-feeding-needy)
3. Ron Legro, In Wisconsin, it's teachers vs millionaires, (http://opensalon.com/blogs/ron_legro/2011/03/04/in_wisconsin_its_teachers_vs_millionaires)
4. Donald Carr, Farm subsidies paid to the members of the 112th Congress, (http://huffingtonpost.com/donald-carr/farm-subsidies-paid-to-112-congress_b_842704.html)

5. Brian Montopoli, Cost of Repealing Health Care Reform Estimated at $230 Billion over 10 Years, (http://www.cbsnews.com/8301-503544 162_20027568-503544.html)

6. Algernon Austin, Paul Ryan's Budget Plan: Trillions for the Rich, Pain for Everyone Else, (http://www.huffingtonpost.com/algernon-austin/ paul-ryans-budget-plan-tr_b_847984.html)

7. Stephen Foster, House Republicans Pass 'Let Women Die' Bill, (http://www.addictinginfo.com/2011/10/15/house-republicans-pass-let-women-die-bill/)

8. Most Americans Say U.S. Headed in Wrong Direction, (http://blogs. wsj.com/economics/2010/01/04/most-americans-say-us-headed-in-wrong-direction)

9. Obama created more jobs in one year than Bush created in eight, (http://thinkprogress.org/romm/2011/01/08/207311/obama-created-more-jobs-in-one-year-than-bush-created-in-eight)

10. Obama's Achievement Center, (http://obamaachievements.org/list#top)

11. Employment Situation Summary, (http://www.bls.gov/news.release/ empsit.nr0.htm)

All My Children

1. Obama Gets Age of His Own Daughters Wrong, (http://www. realclearpolitics.com/video/2011/06/29/0bama-gets-age-of-his-own-daughters-wrong.html)

2. Too Much Vacation for Congress?, (http://ethicist.blogs.nytimes. com/2009/08/03/too-much-vacation-for-congress/)

3. For Obama, A Record on Diversity but Delays on Judicial Confirmations, (http://rssbroadcast.com/?p=59636)

4. Travis Waldron, As Obama Floats Unpopular Spending Cuts in Debt Deal, Cantor Refuses to Budge On Revenue, (http://thinkprogress. org/economy/2011/07/07/262369/as-obama-floats-unpopular-spending-cuts-in-debt-deal-cantor-refuses-to-budge-on-revenue/)

5. Jeffrey Jones, Congress' Jobs Approval Rating Worst in Gallup History, (http://www.gallip.com/poll/145238/Congress-Job-Approval-Rating-Worst-Gallups-History.aspx)

6. GOP congressman heckles Obama during health-care speech, (http://politicalticker.blogs.cnn.com/2009/09/09/cnn-confirms-rep-wilson-the-congressional-heckler)

7. Aliyah Shahid, President Obama's jobs speech: GOP Rep. Jeff Landry of Louisiana holds sign 'drilling equals jobs,' (http://www.nydailynews.com/201109/09/news/30157537_1_moratorium-on-deep-water-drilling-jobs-plan-new-offshore-drilling)

8. Rebecca Stewart, GOPers speak up, but some won't show up to Thursday speech, (http://politicalticker.blogs.cnn.com/2011/09/08-gopers-speak-up-but-some-wont-show-up-to-thursday-speech)

9. Congressman Cantor Caught on Camera, (http://www.wtvr.com/wtvr-cantor-texting-during-obama-speech,0,6447077.story)

10. Rep Lamborn apologizes after 'tar baby' remark, (http://www.cbsnews.com/stories/2011/08/02/national/main20086724.shtml)

11. Richard Cowan and Andy Sullivan, Republicans walk out of budget talks over taxes, (http://www.reuters.com/article/2011/06/23/us-usa-debt-cantor-idUSTRE75M3SA20110623)

12. Peter Grier, Obama versus Boehner on jobs speech date: Who's the adult?, (http://www.csmonitor.com/USA/Politics/The-Vote/2011/0901/Obama-versus-Boehner-on-jobs-speech-date-Who-s-the-adult)

13. Bob Cesca, Convenient Patriotism, (http://bobcesca.com/blog-archives/2009/03/convenient_patriotism/)

We Voted for That

1. Kathleen Hunter, GOP governors trim state employees' bargaining clout, (http://www.stateline.org/live/ViewPage.action?siteNodeId=136&languageId=1&contentId=15997)

2. Kathleen Hunter, GOP governors trim state employees' bargaining clout, (http://www.stateline.org/live/ViewPage.action?siteNodeId=136&languageId=1&contentId=15997)

3. Jim Worth, "Are Republican Governor's Killing American," (http://02d30f6.netsolhost.com/blog1/?p=3077)

4. States With Strict Voter Photo ID Laws More Than Tripled In 2011, (http://abcnews.go.com/blogs/politics/2011/11/states-with-strict-voter-photo-id-laws-more-than-tripled-in-2011/)

5. Timothy O'Hara, Elections supervisor testifies in voting case, (http://keysnews.com/node/37353)
6. Are Republicans Manipulating Redistricting Software To Thwart Voters Will?, (http://www.beachpeanuts.com/2011/07/florida-gop-manipulating-redistricting-software-to-thwart-voters-will)
7. Renee Montagne and Ted Robbins, Hear of Ariz. Redistricting Commission Fired, (http://npr.org/2011/11/02/141926264/head-of-ariz-redistricting-commission-fired)
8. Nolan Hicks, Expert says redistricting map opens door to lawsuits, (http://www.mysanantonio.com/news/politics/texas-legislature/article/Expert-says-map-opens-door-to-lawsuits-2170772.php)
9. Pennsylvania, Nebraska Republicans want electoral vote changed, (http://www.nola.com/politics/index.sst/2011/10/pennsylvania_nebraska_republic.html)
10. Maine and Nebraska, (http://archive.fairvote.org/e_college/me-ne.html)
11. Nick Baumann, The GOP's Genius Plan to Beat Obama in 2012, (http://motherjones.com/politics/2011/09/gop-electoral-college-plan-beat-obama-2012)
12. Judy Ettenhofer, Russ Feingold: Supreme Courts Citizen United discussion was 'recklessly activist,' (http://host.madison.com/ct/news/local/gov't-and-politics/article_9c919aa6-f84c-11e0-a077-001cc4c001e0.htm)
13. McCain Rally Lady "He's An Arab" About Obama Racism, (http://www.youtube.com/watch?v=CjfB1tdC09I)

So It Goes

1. Supreme Court Recount, (http://gab.wi.gov/election-voting/recount)
2. Frank James, Wisconsin Recall Election: All That's Certain Is Big Money Inflow, (http://www.npr.org/blogs/itallpolitics/2011/08/08/139126454/wisconcin-recall-election-all-thats-certain-is-big-money-inflow)
3. Albert Darling Defends Walker's Tax Cuts for Wealthy Wisconsinites that make up only 1 percent of our population, (http://democurmudgen.blogspot.com/2011/08/alberta-walker-defends-walker-tax-cuts.htm/)
4. SJGulitti, Scott Walker, Conservative Hero Propped Up By The Koch Brothers, (http://ny.firedoglake.com/sjgulitti/2011/02/23/scott-walker-conservative-hero-propped-up-by-koch-brothers/)

It's Racism, Seriously

1. Halliburton Iraq contract queried, (http://news.bb.co.uk/2/hi/business/29500154.stm)

Turning in the right Direction

1. David Bornstein, Innovation for the People, by the People, (http://opinionator.blogs.nytimes.com/2012/02/22/from-the-white-house-incentives-to-innovate/)
2. Employment and Unemployment Among Youth Symmary, (http://www.bls.gov/news/release/youth.nr0.htm)
3. GJ Beckus, Banks may not be able to produce the mortgage note, (http://blogs.floridaforeclosurelawyer.org/2009/12/15/banks-may-not-be-able-to-produce-the-mortgage-note/)
4. Romney: job recovery too slow under Obama, (http://www.youtube.com/watch?v=fxQJS2VfpBY)

Let's Pretend

1. Stacy Curtain, Corporate America Pays a Lot Less in Taxes Than You Think, (http://finance.yahoo.com/blogs/daily-ticker/corporate-america-pays-lot-less-taxes-think-125020207.html)
2. Republicans call for lowering, eliminating federal minimum wages, (http://www.examiner.com/democrat-in-los-angeles/republican-all-for-lowering-eliminating-federal-minimum-wages)
3. Administrative Costs of Private Accounts in Social Security, (http://www.cbo.gov/doc.cfm?index=5277&type=08sequence=1)
4. Romney on Immigration: I'm for "self-deportation," (http://cbsnews.com/8301-503544_162-57364444-5035444?)